Welsh Poetry Competition

The Third One

An anthology of the winning
entries from 2017-2021

Editor
Dave Lewis

Publish & Print
www.publishandprint.co.uk

Published by www.publishandprint.co.uk

Special thanks to Kathy Miles, Sally Spedding, Mike Jenkins and all those who've entered and supported the competition over the last fifteen years – you've been fantastic!

ISBN: 9798536804261

Book cover design: Dave Lewis (@radhiphang)
Cover image: Tamanna Rumee

Websites:
www.welshpoetry.co.uk
www.david-lewis.co.uk
www.sallyspedding.com
www.mikejenkins.net

"My proper education consisted of my liberty to read whatever I cared to. I read indiscriminately and all the time, with my eyes hanging out like stalks."

— *Dylan Thomas*

CONTENTS

Introduction 1

The 2017 Winners

Airlings by Rae Howells 5

Skimmers by Jane Burn 7

On watching a lemon sail the sea by Maggie Harris 8

Judge's comments 10

Specially Commended, 2017

Ten Minutes by Natalie Ann Holborow 17

Hare on the lane by Louise Wilford 19

Sunflower Encolpion by Mara Adamitz Scrupe 21

Bergamask for the Neoplatonists by Mick Evans 23

Bones, not human by Caroline Davies 25

The art of moving a piano into an upstairs flat by Kittie Belltree 27

lost poem by Mick Evans 29

Otters by Gareth Writer-Davies 31

In the Bowes-Lyon Museum by Pat Borthwick 33

Running by Natalie Ann Holborow 34

Cawl by Mari Ellis Dunning 36

desert sculpture by Mick Evans 38

Rough Magic by Noel Williams 40

The Wren by John D Kelly 41

Top Corris by Zillah Bowes 43

Grip by Mick Evans 45

Bluebeard by Helen May Williams 47

The 2018 Winners

Prayer to a Jacaranda by Judy Durrant   51

Heft by David J Costello   53

The Mole by Jean James   54

Judge's comments   55

Specially Commended, 2018

Chatter and Requiem by Dena Fakhro   63

All things bright and beautiful by Judith Drazin   65

Breaker by Louise Wilford   66

After Easter by Aoife Mannix   67

Thessaloniki Station 1943 by David Crann   69

According to Dai by Vicky Hampton   70

Division of the Chaff by Sheila Aldous   72

A Clock Full of Coal by Neil Gower   74

Thorsteinsskàli, Iceland by Christopher M. James   75

Wearing Silk Pyjamas in an Aldershot Hotel by M V Williams   77

The Boiling Point for Jam by Lynda Tavakoli   78

From Vivienne to her Tom by Helen Cook   79

Colouring in the Elephant by Sue Moules   81

where he lay undiscovered by Deborah Harvey   82

bonnie dearie by Sighle Meehan   83

The Party by Laura Solomon   84

Swansea Son by Laura Potts   85

The 2019 Winners

The Map-Maker's Tale by Damen O'Brien   89

The Devil's Shoes in *Back Home* Afro-Caribbean Shop   91
    by Pauline Plummer

What are you owl by Rob Miles   93

Judge's comments   94

Specially Commended, 2019

Bob Dylan waits for the Ferry at Aust by Deborah Harvey   99

Making and Mending by Gill Learner   100

The Enchantment of Maps by Jean James   101

Abandoned by Jackie Biggs   103

Frost at Lighthouse Beach by Partridge Boswell   105

Marked by Trudi Petersen   106

Speak by Gareth A Roberts   108

Sestina: The Boxer by Alex Hancock   110

The Promise of Elsewhere by Louise G Cole   112

Ireland is Here by Noel King   114

Dockers 1930 by David Butler   116

Waiting for Gold by Sheila Aldous   117

Mermaids, and where to find them by Karen Hill   118

My mother's heart by Phil Coleman   120

The Archangel Dreams by Peter Wallis   121

Ebb Tide, Morecombe Bay by M V Williams   122

The Red Kite by Barry Norris   123

The 2020 Winners

The Debt Due by Sheila Aldous — 127

To Paul Celan by Linda M James — 129

Unscythed by John Gallas — 130

Judge's comments — 131

Specially Commended, 2020

Hidden Prey by Sheila Aldous — 139

Listen To Me I Am Odile by Judith Drazin — 141

Cell by Helen Cook — 142

Circumnavigation by Sharon Black — 143

A Kind Of Music by Isobel Thrilling — 144

Total Immersion by Konstandinos Mahoney — 145

Mother Goddess of Netherby by Susan Szekely — 146

Moths by Sheila Aldous — 147

In The Gents At Craig-Y-Nos Visitor Centre by Phil Coleman — 149

Delft by Tanya Parker — 150

The Prettiest House in the Street by Rebecca Palmer — 151

A nut roast arrived by Simon Mandrell — 152

Little Pinches (Grandmother's Skates) by Chris Kinsey — 153

Welsh Bamboo by Mike Pullman — 155

Qasida in time slowed to the rhythm of cats by Dena Fakhro — 156

Chosen by the Sea by Jolie Marchant — 157

Large Hotel by Robin Muers — 159

The 2021 Winners

iii by Estelle Price   163

The Yellow Light by Sheila Aldous   165

The Foundling Mothers List Of Pain by Jane Burn   166

Judge's comments   167

Specially Commended, 2021

Shoes And An Old Woman Who Once Lived In Them by Julia Usman   175

Entertaining Caravaggio by Julian Bishop   176

Women of Birkenau by Bex Hainsworth   177

This Shy Architect by Dena Fakhro   178

Modigliani Answers His Critic by Sheila Aldous   180

Consoling The Whims Of The Tiniest, Whiniest
  Dictators by Jonathan Greenhause   181

The Milkmaid by Sally Russell   183

Rebel Song by Jean James   184

A Mural For 'Kitty' Wilkinson by Philip Dunn   185

Lick and Split by Sally Russell   186

Becoming A Saint In Ely: A Speculative Life by Pamela Job   187

The Rev'd Thomas With Scythe, Manafon by Ross Cogan   189

My Shameless Lips by James Knox Whittet   191

Daughter Of The Sea by Miriam Mason   193

Steatoda by Mark Totterdell   195

Blood Lines by Gwen Williams   196

Index of titles   197

Introduction

OK, now I really am starting to get scared. Back in 2007 I thought I'd organise a small, local poetry contest, that might uncover a few decent Welsh poets that had been overlooked by the arts establishment in Wales and that would be about it. If someone had told me then that in a short period of time we'd be the biggest poetry competition in Wales and known throughout the world for running a fair contest that discovers and publishes some of the best poets around I wouldn't have believed them. But here we are, fifteen years later and still going strong. This, despite the many obstacles put in our way by those who get millions of pounds of taxpayers money and whose job it is to help us!

From the start I wanted passion. Once more with feeling. I wanted Barry MacSweeney, Dylan (both of them), Shelley, Bukowski, Tom Petty, Chris Torrance, Kurt Cobain, Neruda, Heaney, Patti Smith, Anne Sexton, Eliot, Pound, Lou Reed, Byron, Gary Snyder, William Carlos Williams, The Clash, *the beats*, John Evans... Yay we got him! Yep, our judge for the first two years and a few more since. Welsh writer, poet, filmmaker, ex-punk rock star, wildlife campaigner and environmentalist, John Evans, kindly agreed to pick the winners back in 2007 and we haven't looked back since.

And so the controversy began. Our very first winning poem, from Gavin Price, wasn't to everyone's taste, but surely the critics missed the point. If we get offended in this life it should be because someone dropped a bomb on some kids not because someone used foul language to describe it in a piece of writing. Being hit with a big stick hurts more than being verbally abused – believe me I know.

In subsequent years we've had other equally powerful poems that can be found in all three of our anthologies. I've lost count of the number of sheer moving poems that have been posted through my door or dropped into my inbox this last decade and a half but every year the old tear ducts get a good cleansing as your heartfelt words burrow deep into me each spring and I emerge each summer hopefully wiser for the experience.

***

1

Many people have told me that the 'Welsh Poetry Competition' has been a breath of fresh air. Particularly in Wales (as well as beyond), as we always seem to get what we ask for - great poems; nothing more, nothing less. We don't filter entries, we judge anonymously and that is it. Just ask any of our judges how we do things and they will tell you, 'Oh yeah, Dave just turns up one day with three or four carrier bags of paper and says: *Here you are, give me twenty awesome poems back.*'

In our third poetry anthology we have, IMHO some of the best modern poetry by some of the best poets in the world. A big claim you might say but I dare you to find a modern anthology with as many great poems. As many of you know I write a little myself, *occasionally* thinking I'm not such a bad poet. And one thing I do know – if I was allowed to enter and ended up in the Top 20 one year, then I would be immensely proud and consider myself to have truly 'made it' as a poet! Such is the high standard of winners our fab judges unearth each year. Long may it continue. And so once again, a massive thank you to all those who enter and make this possible.

***

At the time of writing we have had entries from forty countries, which makes us truly international. This anthology, like the others, will no doubt soon be found on bookshelves all over the world. I even saw a copy of our first book in Windhoek, Namibia a few years back! The power of the Internet, social media and word of mouth has indeed taken our message to the four corners of the globe.

We still get no grants, sponsorship or funding from the 'arts business' in Wales or any other external agencies. We are lucky to have judges that really care about poetry as an art form rather than those who see it as a way to further their careers or earn a few bucks.

And lastly I should also say, 'thank you' to all the poets who so readily gave permission for their poems to be included. The anthology itself has poems divided into years, arranged winners first, followed by the judges' comments and then the specially commended entries. I hope you enjoy ☺

Dave Lewis, October 2021

The 2017 Winners
Judged by Kathy Miles

Airlings *by Rae Howells*

Somebody has wrung them out
two old flannels
two un-eyed rabbits
as if the rain had hooked them from the air
twisted their lives out
wrung them out
two old flannels, loose knots
flung on a heap

flung
on a temple of old bracken
and dry grass, moving,
shushing, *shush*,

or are those fierce whispers
urging wake, wake,
remember?

remember how you ran
into the air,
you could hardly keep your feet,
barely pricked the soft pasture
as you leapt, always trying to free yourself,
flinging yourself skyward

your face turned towards light

but dragging the needle's thread
        the heavy gold thread of yourself
you buttoned your soft weight into the rising of the hill,
paused to press down the ploughed soil with your feet,
small brown pin.

I see now, you were the earth's beat,
her quick blood,

submitting to the arteries of the burrow
only for your dreams of the wind

among warm bodies strung, beads along the vessels,
rows of ears and feet,
each body a stitch in the seam,
        you hemmed the earth and the sky.

Shush now, shush, old flannels, wrung out on a heap,
your legs stretched long on the old dry grass,
listen how the wind sings,
her longing fingers in your fur as she whispers –
        come little airlings
        unbutton yourselves
        kick the light with your feet
        the earth can hold herself awhile.

Skimmers *by Jane Burn*

He says   *mam*
                    like this
                            He says
for the thousandth time   like   this
He says   *curl your finger*
                    mam
And he facepalms and
        he facepalms at my
                plonk
                plink
                plunk
He says   *mam   Epic fail*
and he sets   a pressed   flatbread pebble
loose upon the river   and
                            it
                        bounces
                                five
                                    times
before giving up momentum   becoming
        sunk   He says   *mam*
curl your finger round like you're holding
a tiny baby   He says
mam   at least   you're good at finding them
the skimmers   and I am   I am good
at rooting out these perfect   skin-smooth   discs
like a truffle hog   when I place them
in his palm   he smiles as if   every time
is the first   time   He says
                mam
                    good one
                        Then
                            sets the
                                captives
                                    free

On watching a lemon sail the sea *by Maggie Harris*

and I'm singing 'You are my sunshine' thinking
of my childhood across the sea of incubation
go Honey go
you self-contained cargo ship you
with your sealed citrus juices and pitted panacea of seeds
braving the collision of tankers and illicit submarines

      .they called me *scurvy.*   the lemonade
       my mother made was iced and sprinkled with
             Demerara
(of course)

and I'm wondering, did they grow you there, o lemon mine
you
for your juices
a lemon plantation not to be confused with
a plantain plantation even a banana just don't mention sugar
stack you in the gloom like hereto mentioned bananas
green and curtailed in their growing or even
those force-ripe mangoes with girls' names
nobody knows here and who leave their sweetness behind
bare-assed on the beaches
come
to the marketplace
comatose .

I do not remember lemons, but limes.

    M
  I   E
L   S.

Piled high in their abundance. Limes.
Acid green pyramids on market pavements
holding their secrets beneath their reptilian skins.

And there is my aunt, her arms thin as bamboo
gathering the fallen from the yard, sweeping
their dried leaves into the remembrance of herself
whilst the black maid slips slivers of lemon into a split
-bellied fish whose eyes glaze up at the sun.
Gauguin, you can come in now, remember Martinique
hue the *native* in all her harnessed beauty
the slack –jawed fish, browning blood
the textured landscape in shades of pawpaw and indigo.

But, *liming* is what my lemon is doing now,
(in the West Indian sense), hey ho.
over the waves at Aberporth, there he blows.

Judge's comments

It has been a real honour to judge this year's Welsh Poetry Competition. And, with over 500 entries, a somewhat daunting task, not least because of the quality of the work submitted. Subjects were wide ranging; love, loss, the failure of relationships, and – as one would expect in such dark political times – anger at the world we live in. Many poems dealt with heart-breaking scenarios: death, the decline of a loved one into dementia, homelessness, war, the refugee crisis. There were also many pieces that focussed on Wales, and I was reminded again of how much wonderful poetry is inspired by the history, culture and language of the landscape around us.

Judging is necessarily a subjective process; but from the start I looked for something different. A quirky style, a new slant on an old subject, a strong narrative voice, or imagery that lifted the poem from mere description into something that truly excited the imagination. It was such a strong field that I read each entry many times before deciding on the final placings: every poet had something unique to say, and I wanted to give every poet the chance to shine. The Highly Commended poems in particular were very close, and all of an extremely high standard, so the choice was difficult.

Inevitably, the poems which made it through were those that kept me awake at night. Poems which tugged at the edges of my dreams, or whose words huddled in little corners of my mind and leapt out when I least expected it. Well done to everyone who entered. It has been wonderful -and humbling- to see so much talent. A huge thank you to Dave Lewis for encouraging and fostering that talent and for inviting me to be the judge this year.

1st Prize – Airlings by Rae Howells

As a first-time competition judge, the idea that the winning poem would 'jump out' at me was something I regarded with more than a little scepticism. But that's just what *Airlings* did: it leapt, bounded, *ran/into the air*, flung itself skyward and crept into my sleep. A pair of dead rabbits on the ground, *two old flannels/two un-eyed rabbits*. And yet the language of the poem lifts it away from that stark, unpromising fact into a remarkable and intensely poignant piece. Here we have a threading: life and death, earth and sky, movement and stillness, the claustrophobic warmth of the burrow and the freedom of running in the pastures above. The rabbits are *the earth's beat/her quick blood*: a meshing of body and land that reminds us that we too belong to both and have the same dreams of escape. The poem has the 'otherworldly' quality of the dream/vision poem – perhaps even the Irish Aisling – with the gentle, insistent narrative voice urging the rabbits to wake from death and *remember how you ran/into the air*.

The imagery is precise and delicate, the whole being linked by the metaphor of sewing, a metaphor, which does not overstay its welcome as many do, but which runs subtly through the piece like a strand of finest yarn:

but dragging the needle's thread
        the heavy gold thread of yourself
you buttoned your soft weight into the rising of the hill
paused to press down the ploughed soil with your feet,
small brown pin.

Lines are as beautifully and carefully stitched together as the rabbits packed into the burrow - *beads along the vessels* – hem earth and sky. I particularly loved how the repetitions –*shush now, shush, old flannels* – gave a quiet, lyrical authority to the narrative voice. And at the end, a haunting entreaty to the rabbits:

come little airlings
unbutton yourselves
kick the light with your feet
the earth can hold herself awhile.

A truly wonderful piece, and a more than worthy winner of the competition.

2ⁿᵈ *Prize – Skimmers by Jane Burn*

From the start I loved the confidence and deceptive simplicity of *Skimmers*. A tiny moment in time: a mother and her son skimming stones across the river, the child becoming impatient at his mother's lack of skill:

> *He says*
> *for the thousandth time   like this*
> *He says   curl your finger*
> *mam*

And in his impatience we see the man he will become, the roles already reversed as he smiles   *as if every time/is the first time* his mother taking comfort in the fact that at least she is good at rooting out the right stones.

I love the fluidity of the poem, the shape driving the pace and mirroring the sound and movement of the skimmed stones. The ease with which the lines flow almost disguises the fact that this is a very assured and carefully crafted piece, tightly constructed, and with great attention paid to vowel-play, repetition enhancing the smooth musicality of the lines. It is very difficult to make a child's voice sound natural in a poem, but here the tone is spot on:

> *He says mam   Epic fail*

The language is spare, economical, and yet conveys so very much about the close relationship between mother and son; the child facepalming in despair as each of her stones sink, taking the lead to show her how it is done, congratulating her when she eventually gets it right. At the end the words and the stones skim perfectly, as he

> *sets the*
> *captives*
> *free*

12

Here the child is the teacher, the adult, his mother relinquishing her role for a brief, glorious moment to allow him the chance to enjoy this time of being in charge.

Just beautiful.

3rd Prize - On Watching A Lemon Sail The Sea by Maggie Harris

What initially drew me to this poem, and subsequently made me return to it many, many times over the course of the judging process, was its exuberance, the sheer and absolute joy of its existence. From the first moment when the poet is singing *You are my sunshine*, we are transported to the warm seas and shores of the West Indies and to West Indian/Caribbean traditions of powerful and melodic oral poetry: there is a strong and confident rhythmic voice behind the pen. The central image – a lemon sailing across the sea – leads us to a wealth of remembrances, including memories of the poet's own childhood, and, inevitably, also to the shame of colonialism and slavery.

Yet this is no poem of heavy polemic. The references are subtle, often made in humorous throw-away phrases: *just don't mention sugar*. This lemon is a vehicle, both literally and metaphorically (*you self-contained cargo ship you*), which the poet cleverly uses to hint at those darker aspects of West Indian history. But rather than dwelling on these, she invites us to see it as the vibrant, colourful place of her childhood, a place where mangoes *leave their sweetness behind/bare-assed on the beaches*, and where her aunt, her arms *thin as bamboo*, is

gathering the fallen from the yard, sweeping
their dried leaves into a remembrance of herself
whilst the black maid slips slivers of lemon into a split
-bellied fish whose eyes glaze up at the sun.

The line *Gaugin, you can come in now* made me laugh out loud. At the end, the lemon is *liming* over the waves at Aberporth (in the West Indian sense, a sharing of food, drink and conversation). Vividly descriptive, tender, full of passion and colour, this is a celebration, a brave, glorious hug of a poem. A real triumph.

Kathy Miles, July 2017

Organiser comment

Once again our judge, Kathy Miles, found that this year was an especially good one with many poems being in contention for the Top 20. And so, in keeping with our aim to recognize as many poets as possible I've taken the liberty to include the names of the poets and poems that Kathy singled out for praise but who didn't quite make the final cut.

Special mentions

To The Bay – *Gareth Alun Roberts*
Swan Feathers – *Eve Jackson*
Standing Stone – *Mick Evans*
Observance – *Peter Wallis*
Aberfan – *Mari Ellis Dunning*
Garden startled – *Roger Elkin*
Tarot Cards – *Louise Wilford*
Items Found in Samson's Field – *Ellie Rees*
Tillage – *John Baylis Post*
A Mother-in-Law Yoke – *Philip Burton*
in the dens of the fires swept clean – *Mara Adamitz Scrupe*
The harpsichord in the cage – *David Hart*
Coach Trip to Llandudno – *Gene Groves*
Goat Farms of Maine – *Paul Newser*
In Shukkien Garden – *Glen Wilson*

Dave Lewis, July 2017

Highly Commended, 2017

Ten Minutes *by Natalie Ann Holborow*

    · Grace counts a knuckle
for every minute,
the dull thud of his pulse
    in her hand.
Wedding bands
    stiffen their fingers.
Time scatters--
    one minute,
        two minutes,
            three--

the guard puffing clouds in his collar.
Stars cram above the Liffey
where children crouch
    or scuttle back home
to the dark. Ash rain.
Smoke-signals
    --four minutes,
        five minutes,
            six--
the rivers bend and kiss.

~

In Kilmainham we bent
shivering in the doorway,
    palms pressed in the other's hand
and saw in the stone
Joe on the floor with a blanket
pulled round him like earth,
    a candle stuttering grace.

~

For ten minutes,

we walked between gallows,
     sad crosses
rising stark
as two pole-stars
      --seven minutes,
          eight minutes,
             nine.

A soldier stands by
     with a fixed bayonet,
prowling the edge of his watch.

Hare on the lane *by Louise Wilford*

Driving home, late-evening, early summer - owl-call
and the scent of bluebells still snaking through our thoughts –
we spot him,

        pinned by the headlamps to the gravel verge,
head up, eyes alert. Behind him, a field of rape gleams
like a pirate's treasure

        through a gap in the hawthorn,
under the wide white moon. We miss him by a hair's breadth,
a hare's breath,

        swerving round a red-faced pheasant
strutting a stupid zigzag down the ashphalt. He
had been invisible, dissolved

        like a witch's cantrip in the greys
and browns - but now he snaps into view: wild-eyed stare,
nose mid-twitch,

        whiskers gleaming silver wires,
eyes onyx beads, the white curved edge of his ears mid-turn
two blades of light

        in the gloom. Flash of silvery chest as he rises -
long-legged turn - crouch - swift, low leap through a hole
in the wiry scrub,

        somehow that soft fur not snagging
in the hedge's sinews, somehow that warm body vanishing
in a lost moment

        like a pale flame. Gone. The car has stalled.
A ripple of fluttering sparrows rises, falls. The pheasant
has swaggered off.

A wrinkle of breeze through the beeches,
then snicker and jolt of the engine as we drive on, in silence,
down the pot-holed lane,

harebrained.

Sunflower Encolpion *by Mara Adamitz Scrupe*

she's thinking about   art
triple tulips/ wiry - stemmed cruciformed & curling splendid
  tendrils   once traded fever - mad like money
   or an exceptionally vivid Dutch tile: two
entwined/ afloat in a flat - bottomed boat or antique

   Persian carpets or nakshe/ gold - embroidered kantha -
stitched trousers she'd wear/ teasing; a woman brings
  the thread to the needle a man brings the needle
to the thread/ she's thinking about ingress & egress/ vents
& voids/ breach & burrow she's already been

   to the so – called sanctum/ delicious done
circus tricks on her back on her tummy/ squalls &
  storms make her think of that blonde girl's recital
    hiked up in a champagne
shift cello squeezed between her thighs/ tight/ head thrown

back/ ecstasy   catch & collect
  she's thinking like a petal/ a pistil she is
flower - full / ochre - pollen - smudged density &
  emboli but quandary too   watching

a woman's practiced mouth mime *suck*
  (poppet eyes trained on the camera) OR
some heathen goddess painted as odalisque Roman slave
  girl dirt scraped from licked skin/ oil
spread on shoulders 'til they shone (she's touched

  places she couldn't even see) she thinks
  about genus & species of probe
& separate divide & analyze   & categorize/ she's
  transient a doppelganger the show - stopper

sunflower *Helianthus maximilianis*

multi - partnered escapader   plundered/ captured
by bandits & helpless   she's learned the Norse for
penalty/ a walk over red-hot iron/ rue &

fetter/ one breaks against   the other in fuck - buddy
        bedlam her lands denuded her trees burning
pyres she's learned   vindauga   =
              wind's eye   watching the lens   she's

counterfeit her insides touched   encolpion/ her relics
        buried deep in a silver - tissue - wrapped
case/ in a scabbard's   chape/ the thin bronze pin
        of a belt buckle's   tightening

Bergamask for the Neoplatonists *by Mick Evans*

Any attempt to describe "the Good" would be ... to include it among the beings to which "thus" is applicable. - Plotinus, trans John Gregory in "The Neoplatonists"

how they sustained it
put on music
sat it out in pairs
straightened pillows dead-headed flowers
and hid the husks
                     as connections crumbled
wetting cracked lips
trying not to hear
the secret resentments
desperate and mouthing
in shoals like poisoned fish

and never fully readied for
out of nowhere shards of clarity
and the twitch of fingers in tempo
that meant she still harboured options
on spring's full throated outbursts

but it was over sooner
separated only by otherness
from the red blink of the cd's zero

to salve the news we unstacked shelves
cleared corners
dusted off and played old vinyls all afternoon
slipped back through the jazz age
outside was sleet
street lights glossed its yellow melt
and that was all

but come night's renderings
to assert the good

in the redeemed space
like this you said
and tried to teach me what you learned
in dance class
                we steered clear
laughed off my clod-footed tripped beat
mis-step wrong turns
                   and
paused in hold
through the weighted silence between each track
thought what it is to move
among the beings where song prevails
and perfect abstracts still apply

Bones, not human *by Caroline Davies*

You are dog. Here is your skull
a rich-red autumn leaf brown.

The archaeologists seeking Saxon remains
have dug a metre down in my garden.

Then they find you and the call goes up
"Bones, not human."

Gently they excavate you
with your bones intact, lifted one by one.

You have a 'finds' tray of your own,
separate from the pieces of pottery.

You are back in the afternoon sunshine and the scents
of hawthorn and bluebell to tell you the season.

But you no longer have your senses
so I quest the moving air for you.

You are spaniel sized and I imagine you in your prime
fetching prey with your soft mouth.

Your coat glossy as a conker
and after dark you'd find a place to curl up

near the fire, ever hopeful
of some left-over meat.

Further down they find a larger bone
from an ox or cow.

At the end of the afternoon the pit is filled in
with barrow loads of sifted soil.

All is back to how it was
except you are out and no longer buried.

Your tray of bones is carried away
to be carefully washed and labelled.

If you were human we would give you,
unknown Saxon dog, a proper reburial.

The art of moving a piano into an upstairs flat *by Kittie Belltree*

In the time it takes to switch on my phone
it's already on Youtube. Mark, the JCB driver
mimics my anxious face as he climbs into his cab.
This morning he lifted a static caravan

a rust-gnawed Renault Trafic
and an old school bus before breakfast
my husband says. I'm a worrier.
I gulp as Mark nods him to slip

two flimsy-looking loops
over the front forks, felling
the neighbours' wall with a just a tap
of those titanic tyres as he reverses.

Passengers from the Poppit Rocket
give up their seats as the Old Joanna puffs out
two decades of dust, quavers, creaks then she's up –
Faltering at first the way a lilo fills

after winter in the loft – then she wings
over the bent-back heads of eyewitnesses
aiming mobile phones, my screams swamped
by the holiday traffic honking choc-o-bloc

up and down the street as she soars –
then snags her brass bun feet in telephone wires.
I shut my eyes and try not to think
about half the village with its Broadband down

or what happens to those tacky soft toys
swung from the crooked jaws
of some sly fairground goody-grabber.
I open them as a lorry driver leaps out,

shares a laugh about Laurel and Hardy with my other half
while she hangs like a coffin rocking on air
they take hold of my washing pole
and length of two-by-two.

lost poem *by Mick Evans*

something about a bridge a meeting
day melting into evening
the river's unquelled reflection

strands of memory
twining through the pale wash of sky
figures emerging through torsions of perspective

an exchange of words touch
and steps echoing on stones
a haunting of objects

if not this then ambient light
and colours of the way someone saw this once

something about the reflection
and stones echoing words across lapping water

the callousness of flights of birds
as ripples fragment their passing
and from an open window drift of a nocturne

and landscape focusing the unlimited self
as poem and loneliness
or conversation with distance

and more lucid the stones reflected
and curious lift of the arches the antique lamps
stars pointing the dark flow

and the departures that are something about
the one who leaves creating the one who stays

and how words transform figures at nightfall
into more than silhouettes

and always about letting go
and getting it back our own way

it might have been something about love
or its awakening or your arms' reach against emptiness
or breath and the warmth of flesh

or how the thought finds the word
or the pain as breeze stirs her hair

and something about becoming
and remote and strange integrities
and unreality merging with the fact

Otters *by Gareth Writer-Davies*

for a threesome
the otters are making it look easy
slippery like bars of soap

they swim up river
(the moribund sluice)
that powered one water-wheel

and made someone twenty guineas
whilst otters
moved to quieter waters

it looks like a lot of fun
and if I could join them upon the wash stones in the fast-red stream
I would

stopping only to change my costume
time flows
and the pleasure of skinny-dipping (the dance of the wagtail)

fades
as moiling
I drift onto the sound of the weir

the sparkling cataract
where bones are licked clean
and otters

do not make love on a summers day
but stretch out
upon the balustrade, water-dogs with cheeks full of crayfish

bold tongues
that bring down mountains
I watch from high windows of the felin

the unsleeping stream
that even now
wakes me with romps of otters

In the Bowes-Lyon Museum *by Pat Borthwick*

We gather in a high-ceilinged room. Sun
pours in through tall windows, puddling
deep carpets. Crystal chandeliers shower
down, their lumens tumbling through
droplet cascades of Venetian glass. Almost
everything is still and silent until visitors
assemble round the reticulated silver swan
waiting to hear a dainty chime that sets it free.
We hold our breath. And then it happens.

The swan arches its neck, steers it down
towards the twisted glass rods twirling
in the silvery pond. There are bright bulrushes
and lilypads. A silver dragonfly. A silver frog.
Even a scattering of silver bubbles, each one
finely engraved to enhance its airiness,
capturing and reflecting everything around.
The bulrushes bend in them and the dragonfly
has one etched wing larger than the other.

The swan is moving, its hidden mechanics
groan and rumble beneath the pond. Suddenly
(I think I recall tinkling bells) it plunges its beak
into the water, emerges with a little shiny fish
which wiggles and flaps until the swan stretches
its neck up high. Swallows it. The bells cease.
The swan is inert until the next hour. Not unlike
how our own lives continue in silvery repetition
until it's no longer our turn to perform.

Running *by Natalie Ann Holborow*

must be doing something because
now I'm crying
over the smell of fresh laundry,
the sweet folds, warm, *soft*
as a baby's arse
and the woman
in the garden, tugging towels
from the wind,

    running
past pubs
where someone's father
fossilised on a barstool,
picked beermats
to mosaics. He presses
the wet remains
to his fingertips,
a pad of roughened skin,
but doesn't notice me

    running
through whirlwinds of litter,
tugging my ponytail tight
as the dark thatch
of telephone wires,

    running,
ziplining
the fragile stalk of someone's
tenth cigarette
in a car park,
shielding the struggling
light. It shrivels out
into ashes, whispers
back into the wind

where I'm

                running
to forget
the hollow places,
to forget
the ounce of your life.

Cawl *by Mari Ellis Dunning*

I don't remember the way you held me in the crook
of your elbow, rocked me nearly to sleep, or sung

to ease my grizzling gurgle, and I can't recall
the feel of cloth draped over your arm, a shield

between us, cloaking me from the unknown
dangers that drew red rash across my powered

skin. But I do remember the cawl, the chunks
of chicken, buttery and smooth on my tongue,

and the way you taught me to blow on the spoon
to stop the food from scalding as I nibbled on swede.

I remember the false shoe and the string we used
to learn not to trip over undone laces,

and the time I stumbled and broke clean my collar bone.
I remember times of deep sadness, evenings

of clenched fists and hoarse voices and of not
acknowledging the hurt in your eyes.

I remember home sickness and the longing
when I could no longer smell the heady vanilla

of your wrists, when you became a voice
at the other end of the phone. I remember

the tears that fell from my chin and swallowing
deep gulps of air and your words of reassurance.

and even now, when I sit across the table from you
and feel my eyes skewed with salt, and I squint

through the stream and tell you that my soup is too hot,
that my throat is dry, that I cannot go on,

you purse your lips and show me once again how
to blow until the world is cool enough to swallow.

desert sculpture *by Mick Evans*

Marree Man, South Australia.

in the scorched emptiness
he came to a habitation of gods
fell victim to their diversion

forgot himself and woke unmade
to the knowledge
he must accustom himself

to witness as a bird feel as a man
flex unfamiliar muscles but lament an absence of feathers
out of touch with both his kind

he had only thought to rest a moment
how lonely he must have felt
remembering how was rock was man was bird was air

a last lasting thought
to make something of himself
as he sank to earth

distorted and stretched new crowned
beak faced glint eyed hook billed
fingers tracing -what?- in that mirrorless desert

and how to embrace so much sky
the unscalable terrain's ochres
and bulking threat of rock's grey desolation

convening here birds will formulate religions
lapsing when flight fails as falls of yellow dust
into that irresistible outline

which focuses a nowhere
avian head necessarily turned aside
profiling beak and eye

better to know what we are seeing
the time the place the grief
the old chimera of futurity

predatory he readies himself
but there are other shapings here
an uncreated otherness that he hunts

or hunts him
              but not the pose he would have chosen
just when he thought he was on the right track
minding his business and safe with an identity

comes this unsolicited permanent intervention
of seeing and no avoiding it –
                  We get drawn in
that's the trouble with art

Rough Magic *by Noel Williams*

And when you found a clutch
of stiff creatures behind the Hotpoint,
lumps of old mice and the framework of a frog
you took the flowers from around the house
daffodils from the windowsill and harlequin tulips
laid them on the skip across the soil of corpses.

Or would have, had it been more
than the dream you woke me from
thinking I was writing, finding
me overwhelmed again.
As the days grow shorter you are
more often what you used to be
where I, glancing, in brushing past

in wakefulness, in sleep, am again astonished
and again, how stardust or pollen,
or motes floating as the remnants
of all the dissolved gods and goddesses,
have fused together

like a spell from Prospero
drawn up from the silver core of molten earth
to compose an impossible woman
whose tenderness is habit
whose eyes are open as the morning sea
who rides unicorns to sweep behind the fridge
more herself with every secret
she gives away.

The Wren *by John D Kelly*

It will be finished when the bumblebee hits the windscreen!

I recall his unsatisfactory answer –
at that time – to my question

as today it hits me
once more, when I hear the faintest
yet loudest
of thuds, on a static crystal-clear pane.

It takes me back to the front passenger
seat, of a dangerously overtaking
white transit van, to when I first saw
a life ended in a light-honey-coloured
splat – a suspension
of antennae, fur, wings, legs.

I jump up now
alert, happy to escape the frozen glare
of the still, silent page –
hours of scribbling
producing only crumpled-up paper
to brim the wicker basket.

I slam-dunk another one, throw a useless
pen down on a desk, and bound over
to open the invisible door to see it lying
still, silent on a cold concrete threshold.

Was this tiny featherweight body punched
off course by the icy gale force wind?
Perhaps its druidic spirit simply couldn't accept
the clear alchemy of molten silica, tempered?

41

Did she try to fly through it in a rage?
I lift her – that little bird – the ancient
Celtic sages' friend; no liquid bee or amber
bee-juice on the glass, or even a speck of blood.

Perhaps she's not quite dead, just stunned?
I cup her in my warm hand

      - bring it in -
try to give her the kiss of life.

My lips
seem ridiculous, puckered to a tiny beak.

Top Corris *by Zillah Bowes*

We're close here, clinging to the valley.
Yesterday I prayed to a wood warbler,

on my knees in front of the log burner,
hands blackened, vocal chords chipped:

please, please, just fall down the chimney,
please, please, come on, you can do it...

A bird's all-day struggle is feather tips on slate
and falling dirt. No relief for this new lag until

I open the cast iron for the twentieth time
and a pitch-shine eye stares into mine.

A yellow chest faces me, sugared with coal.
I scoop her - half my palm - into my palm,

roof her with soot fingers, knee the front door
and valley her again. Gone and no one saw,

night blinds down, chimneys sucked by sky.
Only Cader, our quiet mountain.

The robin knows the next day. He's at my sill
as I flick the blue calico, then the lounge below

as I roll up the wicker. Then his stick feet dribble
on the slate block as I unlock the garden window.

I've fallen in with them, the birds and trees.
We all have. I'm the white osprey at the top

of Abercorris, waiting for my pair. I'm the fir
she rests in, a branch crook warm with feathers.

I'm the worn path down to the pool. I'm the newt boating over violet slate. I'm that vast stone too.

Grip *by Mick Evans*

Climb the teachers said so hand over hand
barefoot in vest and shorts rope trick up
                                    to nowhere

and played out topping hands over and above
maddening by turns to slaps
                                    then fists

but an invalid carriage I saw once
muscled along the kerbside the crank going hand
                                    over hand

its black cloak straining shoulders bat winged
and couldn't ungrip seeing's quicksand drag
                                    of gravity

or unlearn the implacable formula
of effort against gains and
                                    that time

watching her fingers curl on the parapet
but seeing the flow and not
                                    reaching out

and the slow labour of years and the forgetting
until the new maths of each
                                    curtailed step

balancing hot angles through hip and wrist
and gauging the weight
                                    and cost

hand over hand of each release
grab halt and
            breath

at each chairback table edge hand hold
towards somewhere
                the pictures

Bluebeard *by Helen May Williams*

In my nightmares, my home looms monstrous.
My hallway mutates to an elaborate cavern;
its columns become animate, tumescent;
stone walls breed excrescent surfaces.
Troglodyte ceilings dwarf my puny stature.

In my nightmares, my ex-wives never leave.
Timber doors dilate, ogives elongate heavenward.
Behind these doors squat conjugal presences:
like fallen angels they endlessly commune
telling tales of labyrinthine emotions.

In my nightmares, the walls are rough-hewn,
the doors are riven oak: then doorways turn
translucent, the finest goat's parchment:
only shadows stop me seeing through them.
Thin partitions conceal the chambers of my past.

In my nightmares, a sunlit antechamber
fills with pious virgins. My ex-wives' busy fingers
ceaselessly text messages to these holy brides.
At eventide starlight shines through arched,
stained windows, to make them blush wide-eyed.

In my nightmares, a black phone rings;
I cradle its globular form to my ear,
listen to tacit whispers,
hear the stained white noise,
haunting pleas dyeing out the blue.

The 2018 Winners
Judged by Sally Spedding

Prayer To A Jacaranda (after seeing 'Wolf Creek') *by Judy Durrant*

jacaranda—lay your mauve-blue bells upon me
as you do the svelte grass
carpet me like a dead body in your dappled-light runnels
– but first
cause gum nuts to swell (in a car boot if you will

that a seed might burst open to crack
merck's cryptic on page 47
roll out cranium's treason all set in plain text
for those of us suffering—brain extraction
or the distraction of a knife in the spine

jack me a hammer to nut out the shell
that almost jekyll and hyde material
that flicks from dull brown to a self-preening
greening putrescence (at the twist of a wrist

tumbleweed's jagged stars—dashed across highways
by prevailing winds before oncoming cars
will know – the propelled to near-fatal odyssey
the vertiginous permanent crumplectomy
the watery turfed-out nefariously
of your hue-skirted blues (before you can even say 'boo!'

so free those captives of blinding 'a-tchoo!'
jump them free from collision
a two-second's indecision a three-day hiatus
– an extortionist's ransom
of limpid black jewel from the dark well's stash
in the safe box of mauve echeveria—will be theirs

[then steeped though they are – in the soft pad of footsteps
in their corridor—i'll make sure
their starkly awoken deep-sleeping depths
are relieved by the dog's breath deceiving]

– only let me
no longer dwell on the rot laid open
in a storm-felled elm
on bougainvillea's butterfly bracts – lying tipped
in a wake where magenta and tracery swim
send a swami – to feather-down me in turban
shroud a five-year-old's tantrum
(red faced and eye popped

but turn—normality's simulacrum
calm demeanour unnerving
back to its flip side where kidnapped and terrified
the mind's thin-glass brink harbours warm-blooded feeling
to where it lies shattered with empathy shivering

raise me neophyte noise
(albeit foot stomp and screaming
from the mire of its burial – its mysterious un-being

from the bromide of alchemy's dearth
let me hug the sobbing—
from three foot six
                    above earth…

Heft *by David J Costello*

Altitude affects them.
Fixes contours in their flesh.
They learn the valleys from their mother's milk,
assimilate the paths' worn ink, the brutal rock,
the hoarse voice of the heather.
Every lamb is impregnated with its map.

Each day the shepherd and his dogs
corral them on the lower slopes
but their internal compass
tugs them back into the heritage of rock,
the heather's cackle,
and the milky-white cartography of snow.

Footnote:
Hefting – the instinct of some breeds of sheep to stay in a small, local area

The Mole *by Jean James*

Little labourer,
sightless in the light.
The sun, our friend,
cannot save you. And the earth,
your chamber, has turned you out,
here, where the edge of the gardens
and the dry-stone walls collide. I see

no wound. Only the wasps speak
of death from your open mouth. I think

of you, solitary in the foisty dark,
small miner with those extra thumbs,
shearing away the weight
of soil until

this dawn. Much later I come back
to find you gone, and in your place

a quickening
where a wreath of pale primroses glazes
the grass.

Judge's comments

This year's Welsh Poetry Competition has yielded another bumper crop, showing bravery, insight and compelling imagery. All human life and more was there. Most poems had something to say, were well crafted with no excess baggage or unintended repetitions, and it was these that nudged towards the light...

To be tasked with being sole judge in such an important, international competition has been an honour, also humbling. I've been privy to the most private of thoughts, taken exciting journeys of a more physical kind, wanting each entry to share something transformative and original, not simply treading old, familiar ground...

Interestingly, most entries used the 1st person singular point of view, with the omniscient aspect rare. The danger was overload, which seemed a tad indulgent and self-absorbed. Less is often more ...

Several ever-popular themes predominated e.g. birds, trees, the sea, loss, ageing, Wales and Welsh legends, memories, birth, relationships. Three poems used pictures as their theme and a handful were set abroad. WWI and WWII also featured, as did present dangers. There were a few villanelles and a couple of haiku. In each entry I was also looking for an 'engine,' not a dribble. Musicality through alliteration and assonance rather than simply chopped-up prose. Instead of well-worn descriptions, those poems that were vivid whatever the theme, mood and setting, internal or external, hit my heart. Each of us is unique, with something different to say, and this competition has again proved it.

Many thanks to Dave Lewis for his support, practical help and encouragement, and congratulations to all those poets who bravely took a chance and whose honed work day by day moved into that light, shining and memorable.

1ˢᵗ Prize - Prayer To A Jacaranda *(after seeing 'Wolf Creek.')* **by Judy Durrant**

I love intrigue; what lies beneath, and this poem's very first lines mysteriously drew me in.

Jacaranda – lay your mauve-blue bells upon me
as you do the svelte grass
carpet me like a dead body in your dappled-light runnels
– but first

Those two ominous words ending a psychotic, pig-hunting loner's plea for that magical blossom to bring him luck and perhaps a woman, pulled me up short. The *entrée* to his dark, anger-fuelled world... In this daring, dramatically constructed poem, we have the unnamed mechanic Mick Taylor, with a mind already in disarray, perhaps – as is hinted – from childhood. A Jekyll and Hyde character who enjoys inflicting the most grievous harm on others yet still weirdly self-aware...

for those of us suffering – brain extraction
Or the distraction of a knife in the spine

The poet eschews punctuation and leaves brackets open, suggesting that nothing is closed. Evil will continue, and so it does until at the very end, the killer feels the need to send for a 'swami' (yogi) to restore order where...

the mind's thin glass brink harbours warm-blooded feeling
to where it lies shattered with empathy shivering

and later, at the end...

from the bromide of alchemy's dearth
let me hug the sobbing –
from three foot six
                above earth...

Everyone has something to hide. Personality disorders abound. This is a sobering *tour de force.*

Note: Wolf Creek is a 2005 Australian horror film written, co-produced, and directed by Greg McLean. Its plot revolves around three backpackers who find themselves taken captive and subsequently hunted by Mick Taylor, a deranged killer, in the Australian outback. The film was ambiguously marketed as being "based on true events," while its plot bore elements reminiscent of the real-life murders of tourists by Ivan Milat in the 1990s and Bradley Murdoch in 2001, both of which McLean used as inspiration for the screenplay.

2nd *Prize - Heft by David J Costello*

From this beautiful poem's simple title and the first no-frills first line, I was immediately drawn into the fascinating and probably little-known world where lambs of certain breeds of sheep, despite repeated upheavals and displacement, are tugged back by 'their internal compass' into

… their heritage of rock.
the heather's cackle
and the milky-white cartography of snow.

I learnt something new from each of this poem's twelve very visual yet deceptively simple lines, empathising with these doomed, young creatures who share with us that universal condition of homesickness. When that perfect last line came, I felt close to tears.

This poet clearly does realise that less is often more and significantly, amongst the many entries coming close to the competition's 50-word limit, has delivered a gem. A worthy 2nd prize winner!

Note: Hefting – the instinct of some breeds of sheep to stay in a small, local area. (to heft.)

3rd Prize - The Mole by Jean James

To many people, gardeners and farmers particularly, the mole is an enemy. Destructive and determined, and yet here the poet eloquently, empathically mourns the death of one found exposed to greedy predators.

This is a powerful, imaginative poem whose economy and originality made it constantly stand out and retain its position amongst many much longer, less focussed entries.

Little labourer,
sightless in the light…

introduces the main character whose mouth is full of wasps, having toiled

… in the foisty dark,
small miner with those extra thumbs,
shearing away the weight
of soil until…

Another parallel to our human lives in often a different darkness yet where toil seems ceaseless. However, the last, short stanza describes some consolation when noticing much later

a quickening
where a wreath of pale primroses glazes
the grass.

Perfectly formed. A worthy 3rd prize winner.

Sally Spedding, July 2018

Organiser comment

This year (like the last few years) was also a remarkably good one with many, many poems being in contention for the Top 20. And so, in keeping with our aim to reward / recognise as many poets as possible we've taken the liberty, this year, to include (below) the names of the poems & poets who Sally Spedding singled out for praise but didn't quite make the cut.

Special mentions

Contours – *Gareth Alun Roberts*
The mouth of the gifthorse is filled with food – *Heather Freckleton*
Ynys Enlli – *Romola Parish*
Electric Ladyland – *Sarah Davies*
Sarah – *Janet Youngdahl*
A stranded sour – *Anne Marie Butler*
Wonderful in every way – *Sighle Meehan*
Old couple shopping in Carmarthen – *Kathy Biggs*
Celtic knot found in translation – *Lizzie Ballagher*
Borges loved these streets – *Gwen Williams*
The texture of snow – *Noel King*
Her diaries – *Roger Elkin*
Mary the pit lass – *Silvia Millward*
1918 – *Shirley Hammond Williams*
The way to mower man – *Phil Madden*
Time machine – *Paul Nash*
Owls – *Gareth Writer-Davies*
Cuttings – *James Knox Whittet*
Milk – *Emma Williams*
Cherries and refuge – *Janet Youngdahl*
The geese fly north – *Nick Bowman*
The tinning – *Heather Freckleton*
Finlandia – *Stevie Krayer*
The godmother – *Lesley Burt*
Items found in Samson's field – *Ellie Rees*
Population control – *Gwen Sayers*

The tiller fields – *Peter Pannie*
Breath – *Anto Kerins*
Revenge of a clockwork orange – *Patrick Jemmer*
Twelve inky years – *Karina Fiorini*
Gansey – *Gordon Aindow*
The flying black pig of Vron – *David Belcher*
Rachael – *Phil Coleman*
Friday preacher – *Ceri Thomas*

Dave Lewis, August 2018

Specially Commended, 2018

Chatter and Requiem *by Dena Fakhro*

Did I remember it right?

I never thought I'd see the Thames
recoil, nor mark the scar

We heard that, like the Ganges
it bore a man
not yet dead but knocked
live and kicking to his tomb

Light a candle

This market, like a busy smudge
Which lengthens the church shadow
Weekly, washing its feet
Of fish guts, offal, sheep's blood
And green leaves fallen from
The crowns of fruit and veg

Today it asks for silence
There is no nectar, no cheese
No sweetmeat offerings
For these are soiled goods
Stamped in fear
Yesterday's waste

London Bridge not falling down but crouching
Gone the gifts from other lands
Spent the purses, still opening
And baring their copper teeth
Yet hushed, silent

Hush, for a minute's silence

What space remains for communion?

When the crates under the arches
Are altar for human flesh and
Butchers' knives knead the hands
Of merchants for unholy war

Stopper the thought, hope it never returns

A night visit from new Rippers
Cracking the pavements
Straining the cobbles
Jumping streets
Like avenging ghouls
Sprung from the Clink
Or another dark history
Unleashed

All Things Bright and Beautiful *by Judith Drazin*

After the war, a threadbare time,
cod liver oil, gelatinous, a single daily sweet
doled out, stout garters leave their imprint
on thin legs, a parcel from the Manor House.
Two pars of knickers with a family crest
slither across the floor, plus fours
gargantuan in ginger tweed stand
stiffly to attention of their own accord.
Newly demobbed my father makes a mock salute.
Tis kindly meat my mother says reprovingly
and look a party dress, it's just your size
now who's a lucky girl,
tomato coloured frills cascade.

The Sunday school encompassed high and low,
mutinous I cower upon a bench,
jam tart, the boy behind me taunts
another gobbles like a turkey cock.
Ignore them says my neighbour
in her well-bred voice, that dress
is vile, I told Ma so, she never listens,
but we can still be friends
look you can share my toffees,
a parcel from America.

Eyes to the front, no fidgeting,
the cracked piano splutters into life.
The rich man in is castle,
the poor man at his gate,
hand in hand we trill,
a little out of tune and indistinctly
for our mouths are full of bliss.

Breaker *by Louise Wilford*

She surfs on a keyboard, bit-lip bright with blood,
left eye shut so she doesn't see how deep the water is.
She chews the insides of her cheeks til her tongue
is metal-sour. Outside, the water bubbles in the back yard,
the lawn a muddy pond; thin seas aggregate in the patio cracks.
The slats of the wooden herb table groan, rosemary
up-ended, plastic pot rocking like a cradle in the gale.
She feels the itch of information labels on her skin,
tight sting of split fingertips from too much washing dishes,
pain in her shoulder from lifting toddlers. She is lost
in a sea-fret of contingencies. She can hear the fog approach.
The ironing mountain staggers to its feet. She won't surf
on the ironing board, refuses to flatten fabric, refuses
to gather up toy cars that mine the room like mousetraps.
Twists her hair til it hurts, scaling the cliffs of her plans,
sledging fearlessly down hair-raising notions that crumble
like snow in her hands. Her shoulders are hunched like a bear.
Knees ache from too many stairs. All she can smell
is old ink and dust, the rusting detritus of junk words
in a scrapyard. She skims the peak of a wave, tipped white
as a hare's ear, crouches and balances, slides down the tunnel
of blue-green saltwater, hearing her own heart's pounding,
the thunder of her breath, the scream of the blood
pulsing through her veins. There's a bruise on her thigh
from when her dreams caught the edge of the dresser
as she passed by. She's not always careful where she treads.
Outside, her car bathes like a hippo in the river of the street.
A cataract steams from the garage guttering; wet litter is pinned
to damp fences like bedraggled bunting; grates overflow.
She can feel her muscles flex, relax - recognises the life
diffusing in threads through her skin as she struggles to rise,
to balance, to stand. She knows she must catch it
before the breaker sinks its fingers into the sand.

After Easter *by Aoife Mannix*

The sun returns.
Shy but confident
in the crown of a daffodil
dressed up as a king,
going to a party with pirates
and superheroes swinging
in a tree house by the owl's island.
Far from the icy rain
of relentless missiles falling
on foaming children
who have no answers to questions
they should never have to ask.

Ariel burns inside her tree.
Her branches not touching
but touched by yellow leaves
too old to know better,
as the birds rebel in their innocence.
Their songs humming in the wind
as if this April were the first resurrection.
These green shoots unsullied,
not twisted in the damp roots
of a hunger so deep
it swallows half the world.

The white blossom in a halo
of green rises up
over the edge of the hill.
Blackbirds celebrate
a morning freshly pressed
as clean sheets on a bed
where you are sleeping,
curled up like a small bear.
Nothing prepared me for
the length of your eyelashes.

Nothing prepared me for
the drone of an aeroplane
skimming the roof tops.
The bombs whisper down
on other people's children.
You say you want to live forever,
like a Time Lord or Jesus.
Your face is the last chocolate egg
hidden in my jewellery box.
I want to promise you
I will always come back,
but I am afraid
of the holes in my hands.

Thessaloniki Station, Greece, 1943 *by David Crann*

In 1943, an estimated 58,585 Jews boarded trains from Greece's second-largest city of Thessaloniki to concentration camps in Poland. To add insult to grave injury, the Jews were forced to pay for their train fare.

We sleep in one room, the *Fräulein*
in another – two rooms beside a platform
at a station in Thessaloniki.

Night. A door uncloses. Hollow feet.
At my woman's urging, I dare my head out.
I glimpse *her* shadow in a waning doorway –
momentarily.

Morning light. I shave fraught stubble
through a scurrilous looking-glass.
My woman scales her teeth.

Day. A door uncloses. Hollow feet.
Carriage doors clap. A guard whistles.
And *her* train creeps southbound –
momentously.

In only moments, guard dogs bray.
Coshes. The lethal shunt of waxen feet.
And our train creaks on Icarus wings north

to melt us far from Thessaloniki…

According to Dai *by Vicky Hampton*

Dai watches the little wheel decant the game's geometry
seeing in its rotation
the old pit head at Blaina.

He said, as miners churned the black below
his grandfather turned red above
belting the descant on Calon Lân with the paint machine round the
   new pitch.
They bled for it see
he said.

Mind you, wives and sweethearts too, Dai said,
wrestled that bitch of sheep-thistled sod;
sleeves rolled with their men in stair-rod sleet to maul
rock and tup and make a playing field,
converting the land of their fathers, which
he said, like God, it didn't want to give up.

His bucket trickles the white,
magnesium as his capped skull, as he trundles, measuring
up
and down

touch line, the half-way, the twenty two...

On that hillside
before each season's spewing of blood and teeth,
his whole line drew them; finicky straight, year in
year out under thunder and blue and buzzards mewing and wheeling
   on uplift,
rickety contraptions squealing on corners at a few zealots
hushed as chapel
watching the virgin marks consecrate,

neat as a peach, Dai said, snow bright

like a line of Blaina valley sheets.

They say, said Dai,
in the Millennium, when they expose heaven,
the wind drops in reverence to groundsmen -
like players, he says, hewn
from the granite of youth forged
in steel and coal.

And he should know. He's a chip off the old block,
drawing his tachometry with love
round the boundaries of their passion.

Division of the Chaff *by Sheila Aldous*

A battle for this rim of earth: propelled
by jets of rain, this arithmetical season,
where Spring is wounded in the ground
in its fight for life –

I count buds ripening on Magnolia,
add up wallflowers after overwintering,
and think of the cold war of nature –
I wonder how some escape.

I see if I don't prepare, wield the spade,
dig the beds in time, masked invaders
with innocent smiles and cuckoo lips
will multiply, settle in,

run amok and smother shrubs, wipe out
flags of peony, heads of antirrhinum,
choke roots of assent, stunning rose,
love-lies-bleeding, be murderers in my midst.

Spring is nature's tooth and claw,
at risk of zealous over-gardening.
Sheds hide skulls crossed with bones,
aimed to kill those not counted out or in.

So weapons sharpened: secateurs, shears,
hedge-trimmers, long-arms, pruning hooks
and axes for slashing, cutting, chopping,
for subtracting and eliminating life.

Spring is arithmetic on a country walk.
I count the ways; the stiles, the hills I climb,
the words the river speaks as it gossips
misinformation, disinformation, illusion.

I calculate an empty field mid-trimester,
tally seedlings planted, still sleepy, in beds,
bunkers, caves, unaware of the laugh
of crows bombing from a gash of sky.

In Spring I hear the farmer load his bullets.
Coldly he enumerates how many he will need
to take the lives of hooded eyes, maggoty
skins, worm-hearted spreaders of a plague.

Vengeance is his: he adopts the phrase
to punish the plunderers from darkened skies
gathering in the service of assassins.
I see he has them by the throat – divided.

He blows away the killing smoke,
counts the corpses in the crop, buries
them in fat-earth graves as his field turns
black to red – and in their place grows wheat.

Chaff and death are just numbers not reported.

A Clock Full of Coal *by Neil Gower*

For Percy John Gower, 1907-1960

A slow burn at four o'clock
where your pitted knuckle
winds each Sunday night;
a tacit rite of love, from the hearth.
For Nancy – all *cariad* and *cwtch*,
whose own taut hands can slice
fresh bread paper thin and wring
shirts all but dry - you turn
the tick into the walls, set chimes
to measure school, fireside baths,
shifts, first pints in The Cwm
"to clear the dust": the run-off
that will settle and build within,
black, by minute and month
to cast you gasping, wracked,
between pit and pendulum
on a makeshift bed in the parlour.
But for now, the boys upstairs,
chain-smokers in waiting,
breathe easy and pull sheets
tight to the tick, the chime;
the chimney breast is warm.

Thorsteinsskàli, Iceland *by Christopher M. James*

"Outlaws fled into the broad expanses of the harsh Icelandic interior...
The general populace came to fear the vast backlands as the haunt
of supernatural evil." Lonely Planet

Blistered-lipped, they ate their horses,
angelica root, the little that was at hand.

Nights, the locked sky swung as gently
as pendants around their necks

when they rocked like autists on lava flows
and gripped their shorn translation of life.

Escaping their revenge killings... inland,
a prison already, why build more?

Smouldering came late to the sky's edge –
too winter long, too summer short, though

bright enough to pick lice from one's clothing –
and snow shrank to laid-out body bags.

How often they scanned the thin horizon,
veins drumming like full regiments,

their optic nerves twitching, jarring –
enough to go blind with the focusing.

Forefathers came, but what grew here
were men remembering being children

elsewhere. Family trees only were planted,
the others cut. Then one plain day

the only way onwards was into myth,
following a cortege of shadows

across the vast, cold hinterland, shadows
of killed brothers, of starved kin,

their minds grinding resentments like bones
into the tiniest of fragments. Earth's

anger was universal, glaciers blackened,
and the tightrope of hunger made them

narrower and blinder. On rare days,
the northern lights' soundless folds

of silk crushed them by beauty
as they fell to their knees.

Wearing Silk Pyjamas In An Aldershot Hotel *by M. V. Williams*

The scarlet paint was peeling in the dingy B & B.
We had picked at greasy chicken in the local KFC
And I was feeling lonely and in need of TLC.
The bed was cold and creaking, with a damp and musty smell
But I wore my silk pyjamas in that Aldershot Hotel.

We watched a Beach Boys tribute band to pass the time away
And the waves came up and hit us as we sat in dumb dismay
In a theatre full of pensioners far from surfin' USA.
And the sound of squaddies fighting, getting drunk and raising hell
Erupted in the street outside that Aldershot Hotel.

And second-hand pornography filled up the bedside drawer
Where lonely men too far from home had spent the nights before
And the small TV's remote control lay in pieces on the floor.
But we were passionate and young, and loved each other well
And I wore my silk pyjamas in that Aldershot hotel.

The shower we shared was dirty, but our hearts were riding high.
There was time enough to worry; there was time enough to cry.
If you return and love me I will know the reason why:
We learned to love each other long before the last farewell
When I wore my silk pyjamas in that Aldershot hotel.

The Boiling Point for Jam *by Lynda Tavakoli*

She is making jam in the tiny kitchen,
aproned up, thumb-worn spoon in hand,
fingertips browned like nicotine
from plums she'd stoned an hour before.

Through the window she watches him work,
his naked back a tease of muscle-bulk
as axe splits wood, big hands tender on the shaft
with every shlurp of the blade's release.

She adds sugar to the softened fruit,
stirs until its coarseness fuses the pulp.
Then she waits. Outside the sky is bruised with cloud,
the day punished for its obdurate cheerfulness.

He stiffens then, minding something beyond her reach,
and in his stillness she finds the man she knew
who measured time with shrugs and rinsed his days
 with promises she could not keep.

Now there is only her raw womb,
the haemorrhage of empty-bellied days
stretching behind her like a barren sky
and the sweet spit of fruit pricking at her skin.

Yet there is peace in the ordinary:
the boiling point for jam, the quiet release of a latch,
the skirting of his arms about her waist,
the hope that love would always be enough.

From Vivienne to her Tom *by Helen Cook*

If only you would come.

My smile gathers dust like
flowers in an empty room.
I dream of
your shadow falling crooked
across my bed
as on a broken wall
my tall American Prince
your voice deep and thrilling muffled
by the fog inside my head
that fights for reason like
crow on dead crow.

Please take a seat
although it is scraped
and tell me
in your drifting way
of things I have passed.
I love to watch your hands
darting in conversation
your eyes that waver from my face
as you speak to one behind me.

Look around
do you like what you see?
Shadows mist the twist of
your poet's mouth
that once spilled
honeyed words for me and me alone
but is muted now.
Your absence reveals the arid plains
of a sand-strewn heart.

For I am one who knows life
is a hurried walk in the dark
and you, dearest, have travelled a separate path.
And when I have whimpered my last sigh
will you be there at the throwing of clod
placing of lillies on a rainy afternoon
wrapped tightly in
your Church's appeasement?
Will you take care that the words on stone
are true?

Go now your visit made
but promise a return.
Departures pinch me.
In this mad house I am numb
my life a hollow carcass
dried stripped bare.

If only you would come
to me your wife -
a child scratching at your door.

Colouring In The Elephant *by Sue Moules*

Ancient animals, endangered
by their ivory tusks.
Elephants walk tail to trunk
linked together, a matriarchal society.

The felt pens are bright
we grab them, are children again
concerned about neatness.
There's silence as we colour within the lines.

Everyone is different, individual.
At school they looked for uniformity,
a way of seeing who would fit within
the lines, who would make the grade.

We colour our elephants every colour but grey,
line them up tail to trunk.
watch them walk away
in a sway of slow movement.

where he lay undiscovered *by Deborah Harvey*

In the never-quite-dark
of those first summer nights
I heard police helicopters sweep overhead
seeking the heat of suspects in hiding
trespassers, burglars, car thieves, murderers,
cannabis farmers

It was blow flies that found me
After the buzzing, lascivious squirms
the memory of rotting plums forgotten in a fruit bowl,
then squadrons of beetles homing in
the family of foxes that fed on my lungs,
the bone of my shin

As for you lot driving past
after tiles for your bathroom, this week's fashion
upgrades for last year's mobile phone
who don't notice me in elders and brambles
on your daily commute to your home,
there's no need for guilt

You've not ignored insects crawling on windows
snowdrifted mail behind a glass door
and I like it here
Already a second year is turning,
I wait for dead leaves to tuck me in, ground frosts
soft as flannelette
                                        untongued, undone
I don't call out

bonnie dearie by *Sighle Meehan*

I held you in the crook between my wrist
and elbow, a hatchling no bigger
than a baby gull, lighter than a kitchen bag of sugar.
I sang to you, old songs from my grandmother
who heard them from her grandmother, a woman
banished from Kintyre
who found a home in Fanad
the how and why of it obscured in family lore;
her face or what she looked like,
the story of her tainted baby,
the way her gaze went back across the sea,
all forgotten

until she came to me when you were born
pre-term, too weak to live,
coaxed milk between your perfect lips
curled your perfect fingers round my breast
called you *bonnie dearie*
told me you were meant to be.

The Party *Laura Solomon*

You have to be dead to be invited to this party.
As is to be expected, all the stars are here.
Janis, Marilyn, Jesus.
There are ordinary people too though.
Kevin Watson who died of a blood clot to the brain
shortly after his 40th birthday.
He's been resurrected. Now he's partying in the corner –
he's put himself in charge of the music
and is playing Nirvana
as Cobain toys with a segment of his blown-off head.

Other run-of-the-mill folk present?
Jimmy Molesworth who hung himself
and is now hitting on Janis Joplin who is oblivious
to the attention, dancing wildly to *Come As You Are*
a whisky bottle clutched tightly in her right hand.

Jimmy's still got rope marks around his neck.

There's Cindy Rutherford who was hit by a car
while simultaneously cycling and listening to her iPod.
Not a good combination. She's got splinters of glass
from the windscreen embedded in her face.

Marilyn decides to re-stage her death for our general entertainment.
She strips off and swallows a bottle of pills.
Then passes out in the bed. Nobody looks alarmed.
It's all faked; we can't die now that we're dead.
The black telephone rings.
I move to answer it.
Nobody is there.
I can hear the 22nd Century heavy breathing down the line.

Swansea Son *by Laura Potts*

He is here in my autumn of age
the riverlight through windowpanes,
the small-hour laughter,
the slim-supple night,
and moonlight eyes on the history page.

I remember his name that giggled the stars
when the stage of the world lit its lights for him,
and I, summer's daughter,
he Swansea's son
whose words in the plash of the water
we hear in the echoes of hills. Still

the ghost in my arms in the cracked black night,
still in stairwells that old grey light that writes
of the deer shaping the dales, that writes
of bonfire-bright half-pint ale, that writes
of Death in His coat and tails:

you, man of words with the firefly eyes,
who didn't stay to see the wild spring flowers
riot on the mountainside, who died
like a steeple that cradles its bones,
and whose voice now sleeps beneath Wales' stones,

you, my lone man with the light, lord of all words,
whether I'm there with you or not, well, that's alright.

The 2019 Winners
Judged by Mike Jenkins

The Map-Maker's Tale *by Damen O'Brien*

She came in through the clatter of the doorway,
behind her the squalling storm like a wave's black tongue

and in her hands a sheaf of maps and mildew
and franked and mothy deeds to lands

long washed out of the way by indifference and
the blue melt and the green gloss of the ice.

I had to tell her that I had no jurisdiction
below the greedy fingers of the highest tide,

that her father's promises and titles had been drowned
when the islands had gone under and the shores

had climbed up the First World's sneer to the hills.
The old lives that we followed have been overturned,

the lines we stood behind with our shields and swords
and told the world it could not take its shelter,

all overrun, all gone into a swallow and
the world's poor wander where they will or not.

She cursed me as a whale might curse a hunter,
as a spear might curse the hand that flung it,

and took back those deeds, the wax and paper
which proved to be a poor seal to the water, to the

welling and washing of her ancestors, the salting of
her ancestors in their lost graves. She warned that

she went to treat with one who owns the water,
that on nights like this I should sit uneasy in my office

where all the lines of yes and no are tangled
and blur and twitch like so much compromise,

for the storm is blowing straight against my door
and it blows the tide behind it to heights before unknown.

She turned and left, her hair wild as the weather, and
where she'd stood, the brief puddle of her leaving

formed a map I have little power to decipher and none
to alter, and by the door, a single sequin scale.

The Devil's Shoes in *Back Home* Afro-Caribbean Shop *by Pauline Plummer*

In between the cardboard boxes of yams,
plantains, green bananas and cassavas,
under a shelf of pilchards, beans
and bottles of palm oil,
a line of men's shoes, asleep
like parrots on a perch.

Are they the devil's shoes? I ask the shopkeeper.
They are multi-coloured leather, slippery as skin,
red, black and beige, or orange, yellow and brown
with long pointed toes, like an armadillo's tongue.

They shout high life and jive
at weddings and birthdays,
sliding and tapping to insistent rhythms.

They flirt in church beneath the sober suit
mouthing, *I am a man who can afford expensive shoes.*
They may be bought by a wad of cash
in the hands of a spoiled son
or paid for monthly by a ticket collector,
and polished with spit and a rag.

These shoes look too often at their reflection
in shop front windows.
They diss worn-out trainers or cut-price shoes.

Pulling back the hoods of their convertibles
they drive off taking the finest girls
from the men who love them.
They wear gold from Dubai
silk shirts and camel overcoats.

But they never walk on a beach at dawn

in awe at a sunrise or tread the
pilgrim's way.

What are you, owl *by Rob Miles*

if not the wind's wild tuner, unherdable
sky cat? Philosopher
my foot, more the quill-swivelling

killer, all plume-roots and iris. They say
your eyes are too big and round to allow

for much mind, but we all know
you're uploading data
to the moon, winging over frost-

groomed trees and tiles. Folk's fly-by-
night cockerel, yes, we find what's coughed

up, we've seen your dirty tramp-troll
earplug-pellets, we know
you've visited from what you've gifted, itchily

relinquished, your tightly
and politely compacted

capsules of grief, the unholy
remains of bony souls you snared
to swallow, to regurgitate as tufted soundlessness

your dinner made dumb and not listening, listening
like us, not breathing, blue-lipped and hushed

since you don't come near nearly
enough, it has to be you, you, you...
or air.

Judge's comments

1st Prize - The Map-Makers Tale by Damen O'Brien

The joy of judging a poetry competition is finding a poem which takes a totally different direction and approach to all the others and the winner's exactly that. Not only is its narrative descriptively intense, but it creates in such a short space, a world you inhabit, albeit a frightening, dystopian one. Curiously, the imagery of maps was used effectively by three very good poets in this competition; but this one handles a grave topic with subtle imagination.

2nd Prize - The Devil's Shoes in Back Home Afro-Caribbean Shop by Pauline Plummer

In contrast, the runner-up is single focussed, describing the shoes in the title and being led by them to a conclusion in the way that poems should best develop, following imagery and not ideas. These shoes take on characters, suggesting dance and celebration and, ultimately, dangerous allure. I love the way they sound so enticing and exciting, yet end with a sense of the hollowness of wealth and superficial attraction.

3rd Prize - What are you owl, by Rob Miles

I was in a quandary regarding third place, but again the sheer power and empathy of this poem was hard to resist. While it owes something to Ted Hughes with 'quill-swivelling / killer', the awe throughout impressed. I especially love the ending, with its onomatopoeia of 'You, you, you… or air.'

Mike Jenkins, July 2019

94

Organiser comment

Yet another outstanding year for entries sees so many good poems being in contention for the Top 20 spots. And so, in keeping with our aim to reward / recognise as many poets as possible we've taken the liberty, this year, to include (below) the names of the poems & poets who Mike Jenkins singled out for praise but unfortunately didn't quite make the specially commended section.

Special mentions

Oh To Be In England – *Emlyn Williams*
Cymraeg – *Rachel Carney*
Arabia Felix – *Virginia Griem*
Simon Says Nothing – *Angela Fish*
Don't Swipe Her Like A Dish Cloth – *Barry Norris*
Superhero – *Sally Festing*
Pots Of Paint On The Roof – *Brett Evans*
100 Hours Of Darkness – *Ashley Chan*
Sister – *Jan Westwood*
These Feet – *Vicky Hampton*
Dachau Carpenter – *John Baylis Post*
In The Maternity Ward – *Ann Leahly*
Accordion – *Pauline Plummer*
Choughs At Llechwedd Slate Quarry – *Sarah Lewis*
Mapped Edge – *Rob Cullen*
Ermine Coats – *Diana Sanders*
In The High Street Charity Shop – *Louise G Cole*
Perfect Pitch – *Christopher M James*
How I Learned To Love Monsters – *Gill Learner*
Trefoil – *Sharon Black*
Brad From Joe Soaps Hand Car Wash – *Roger Elkin*
Cariad – *Gareth A Roberts*
On Newport Footbridge – *Lawrence Illsley*
Tragi-Colours Of Rajastan – *Jeffrey Grenfell-Hill*
She Tries Bless Her – *Geraldine Hunt*
Granny By The Sea – *Judith Drazin*

Flotsam – *Phil Knight*
Direction Of Breath – *Bess Frimodig*
Woken By Words – *Lizzie Ballagher*
The Gypsy – *Dominique Hecq*
Thrush Green – *Sally Russell*
Y Ddraig Goch – *Rowan Kinnear (11 Yrs Old)*

Dave Lewis, July 2019

Specially Commended, 2019

Bob Dylan waits for the ferry at Aust *by Deborah Harvey*

The tide is so far out it's over the horizon.
You are far out too, dressed in black and wearing shades
against the quibbling English rain

Electric Dylan, stalking the slipway
hands in pockets, shoulders hunched
your feathers ruffled

waiting for the ferry to tie up at the pier
your back to the river, facing land
while I frown, trying to work out where you're standing

but the wooden café's rotted, gone,
the moorings silted up with mud,
the turnstile entrance to the Gents rusted shut.

Even the bridge being built behind you
replacing this passage of two thousand years
is underused now, left to drift among the clouds

as the warth fills up with rising water
and a heron straggles into flight,
turns and trails its spindling legs across the Severn.

On 11th May 1966, the American photographer Barry Feinstein photographed Bob Dylan waiting for the Aust to Beachley ferry at Old Passage, Gloucestershire.

Making and Mending *by Gill Learner*

After all the shaping and shifting, the naming,
dividing and gathering, the bringing forth,
he sat at ease, feet up, blessing what he'd wrought.
But midnight skies were blank, so he fashioned
tiny Mercury, diamond Venus, garnet Mars
and others, strung on threads around the sun.
But his jade and sapphire prototype, white-capped,
was favourite, smiled on every century or so.

Time came when he had to peer through haze.
Pleased at man's inventiveness, he vowed to check
more frequently. Quite soon he saw the blue
was streaked with white, green scarred with brown.
He scowled, sent warnings – burst the earth's crust,
whisked the air to fury, made bodies burn with fever –
but the changes speeded up.

Angry, he scanned the heavens, saw Saturn
with its icy rings, plucked one the size of Moon,
shaped it to a lens, held it up to Sun. He watched
the busy creatures panic, shrivel, drop until
nothing breathed or moved. He sent monsoons
to wash the planet clean, restored the caps
with icy breath, refilled the seas, set to work again.

The Enchantment of Maps *by Jean James*

When the dementia was still in its infancy
I would bring out
the map of Ireland
and we would trace old holidays,
crossing the border to a 'foreign country',
through Pettigo, where the uniforms
gave us a green triangle
to show that we were from the North:
an expedition,
the names exotic:
Buncrana and Bundoran
Letterkenny and Killybegs.
You must remember
Rossnowlagh,
that beach where the Atlantic
flung out a driftwood mermaid
I have still.
And we laughed together at
how the creases on the map
were always over places
we wanted to visit,
places you were good enough
to find for us, your children
forever asking 'please' for more.
How often did you stop the car
to tell us stories?
Tales from the old days,
tall I'm sure,
that rattled in our minds long after
we were sent to bed.

Those days are gone,
the real and the imagined,
the map left folded
when you no longer knew my name;

a border crossed,
somewhere no map can ever show.

Abandoned *by Jackie Biggs*

He's on his own throwing stones,
a scruffbag lad on a dusty square
down a deadend street

at the end of nowhere.
He'll target windows
until all of them are blank.

A jagged piece crashes
and smashes into flinty sparks
on a concrete floor –

a small highlight for this
early evening boy
who wants to stay out there

until darkness rises
and the heat of day drops
a grey covering

over ragwort and buddleia
that pokes from cracks
around a small building ...

Door hanging open
roof collapsing
'keep out' sign peeling paint

by a broken down fence
and a useless gate.
'No trespassing' whines

in distorted red and
'DANGER' shouts in crooked capitals
but the boy can't read the signs.

The last complete window
flares like a sheet of flame in glancing sun.
He chooses half a worn brick

hears firecrack of glass
sees the blaze shatter.
He kicks up smoke filled with dust

and heads back towards town
where orange streetlights start to glow
as the sun goes down.

Frost at Lighthouse Beach *by Partridge Boswell*

He's out early with all the other dawn and shell seekers
       imitating wading shanks, treading his own delible barefoot
thread along the backwash of Sanibel sand—puttering

and pausing, stooping for stray sparks of littoral bling
       at his feet, maundering on—the woolen ham of his head
dipped, fixed on what could be periwinkles, sea biscuits

or whelks slipping through the frothy film and spillage.
       He dodders at the surf's effervescent hem, baggy khaki
trousers rolled to his shins, Tommy Bahama luau print

festooned with swaying palms and surfing wahinis splayed
       open to the navel of his barrel chest, turning a liver-tinted
tulip over in his leathered farmer's palm, his ancient lips

imperceptibly kissing each word mumbled under his breath
       heedless if anyone might sense his affection for the waking
light or be the least bit curious in his discoveries, undaunted

by deadlines or lectures or harvests of young unripe minds,
       not wielding an ax-helve or weeding a garden or needing
to justify wedding a vocation with an avocation—just on

vacation, seizing whatever washes up and catches his eye,
       his crenshaw cocked to one side in a crux of amazement
cresting the decisive moment when he almost pockets his

treasure for a shelf or a grandchild's slack-jawed awe
       then tosses it back without a sigh.

Marked *by Trudi Petersen*

Johnny remembers his grandfather's forearms.
Marked, blue scars traced across the sinews,
Parchment skin. Anthracite embedded, worked to the surface,
Picked out with needle and thumb push. *"Black gold"* he'd say.
Never complained, even though his lungs were messed up,
Pneumoconiosis. Could have had worse luck,
Least he made retirement, plenty didn't. That's just how it was

He doesn't remember the closures, just a baby then,
Brought up on stories, down the club at lunchtime with the men.
"Don't you tell the old girl. Oy Shirl, give the lad a half a pint.
I'll keep an eye and see that he's alright."
Change for the fruit machine, a bag of crisps to keep him quiet.
Racing on the TV screen, Maggie's Dream comes in at 25 to one.
No one in there would have bet on that one

Dad; bad back, arthritic knees, on the sick since 93.
Pills for the pain, pills to make him sleep, pills to keep the side
  effects at bay.
They say, *"You will have to go some butt*
To be half the man your Da was way back then".
And they tell him of the time when the roof fell in.
Big Al Evans, trapped beneath the rubble.
"Your Da he saved the day. Leapt in there like superman, pulled him out
the way"

Big Al Evans? gone now, topped himself they say.
"Duw, what a waste" but *"proper hero your Da was."*
And they slap him on the back and raise another glass,
To memories, to Da, To big Al Evans, rest in peace.

It's changed here since he was a kid,
The landscape greened, The river clean,
They talk about regeneration, he's not sure what that means.
No job. There's no jobs for somebody like him.

No cash, no car. They closed the club, there's empty shelves in Spar.
He's still at home with Mam and Da
But this place... this place. God he loves it,

It fits him like a glove.
Family everywhere, cousins by the score.
His auntie Vi lives up the road, his sister lives next door
But this place…this place. God he hates it.
It crushes him, sucks all of the life from him.
He says he'd leave here if he could but he knows he never would.
How could he leave this place?

Love and hate. He blots it out, gets off his face with booze and
    drugs.
First it was the speed and now the smack.
Everyone he bothers with is on it now.
Heroin. It came up the valley like a dam burst,
Drowned whole villages and towns. Arrived here first from
    Liverpool they said,
Now half his mates are dead, O.D's, hepatitis C.
That's just how it is.

Black gold under green. Gold turned to brown. Brown into
    crimson,
Tourniquet twisting. He pushes it in with needle and thumb. Sinks
    into black.
Blue scar tracks, mapped across his skin,
Like unmined seams.

Speak *by Gareth A Roberts*

(with acknowledgement to The Fold of the Bards *in* The Book of Taliesin*)*

It is a fit time to go to the drinking
with the skilful men, about art,
and a hundred knots,
the custom of the country,
the shepherd of the districts,
support of gates –
like going without a foot into battle...

or going home without a tongue,
not knowing the proper speech of stones;
to stir at the cauldron
for its fleetest drops,
labouring a year at the blending;
and the years' flame kindled.

I have shifted shapes for you:
flesh of the river, bone of the sky.
In the dirt I made myself a seed
for your scratching
that you may bear and bare and birth me:
your radiant brow. I am the bastard
that cannot be loved, lord or killed;
a foundling condemned
forever to be found
in the mouths of rivers
and the sea's tongue... a tongue

to cause loquacious bards a hindrance:
a cell, a cleft, a restoration
and depository of song. I am a literary man.
I love the high trees
that afford a protection above,
and a bard that composes

without earning anger.

I am the flower that grows the night,
a mountain beneath your road.
I am pot holes, a tile loosed
and opening roofs to rain
and my voice. I am what is
behind the trees,
behind the light, crowing,
where high places bring
the arduous path.

Sestina: The Boxer *by Alex Hancock*

Noah returned from the corner shop with his cigars and six-pack,
entered the bungalow, slung his damp boots by the unlit fire
and hung up his wool coat, dripping from the stormy deluge.
Swansea hadn't heard such thunder since the war
when the bombs came raining down upon the docks
and the sound went booming and echoing up the valleys.

The front door opened to the tune of rainwater pouring off the roof's
valleys.
"Come in Dai" said Noah, in the fridge shelving the six-pack.
A man entered wearing fisherman's waterproofs fit for the docks.
"Just got in myself" said Noah, "You look half drowned. Let's have us a
fire."
He lit the newspaper, flames surged like raging cannons at war
With the darkness, then moved the guard to keep back the embered
deluge.

"This rain hasn't stopped for days, roads cut off by the deluge,
people stuck in the villages, mudslides in the valleys"
Dai huffed, "Seen nothing like it. Everywhere's closed. It's like we're at
war"
"It's Wales, Dai. It rains. Want a drink?" Noah broke the yoke of the six-
pack,
opened a tin and poured the cool lager down his throat, quenching its
fire.
"Heard you'd had a spot of bother" said Dai, "What's that by there?
Been to the docs?"

"Bother? No, no, I'm fine" said Noah "I was walking past the docks
last weekend, sea brimming over the wall, waves up in a deluge.

Across the Bay Port Talbot was a carnival of fire;
smoke from the chimneys drifting towards the valleys.
Sunday it was, off-license still open, boys on the street with a six-pack
enacting their brother's tales of Wind Street on a Friday night -
    prowling for war.

They started shouting "grandad this, drunkard that". Even mentioned
    the war.
"Off you trot now, boys" I said. "I used to work the boats on the docks."
"Now you piss yourself, you old cunt" said one. They followed me, this
    six-pack
of youths up past the pub, then attacked. Blood spilled onto the
    pavement in a deluge,
and flowed into the gutter like streams down the side of valleys.
My cigar rolled into a pool of crimson and went out with a tiny flicker
    of fire."

The hammering on the roof stopped. Noah looked out of the window
    at the fire
in the sky. The firmament stretched out like a vast battlefield with The
    God of War
watching over the Bay's electric-lit hills and the ripple of valleys,
and the Channel with its twinkle of cargo ships sailing to foreign docks
and the lamps of cars spilling off the motorway in a deluge,
fizzing past. Noah cracked opened another tin from the six-pack.

"Towns in the valleys harden those lads; unemployment, boredom
    gives them fire.
Fuelled with a six-pack and they're hungry for bloody war.
They'll end up in the dock but might behave after my fists rained upon
    them in a terrible deluge."

The Promise of Elsewhere *by Louise G Cole*

When you are arranging my funeral,
gutted at the finality supposing death,
stunned at the shock of our parting,
try to find a physicist to explain how

I'm not really gone, that I am still here
and there, elsewhere and somewhere,
not in the way of blind faith in heaven
or hell, not even languishing in purgatory

but still here in this one universe where
everything is energy, and all the photons,
particles, atoms, neutrons, neurons making
me, only me, still exist, by the laws of science,

cannot be destroyed, as all there ever was,
is now, will be for ever more, measured
across the continuum of time and space
by scientists, explained by physics, the

soft touch of my skin, the blue of my eyes,
the thumping heartbeat, that special smile
I always kept for you alone, this property
of the cosmos keeps going, every vibration

that was me is still here, now it continues,
my one being pulsing through a universe
so profound, where no energy is created,
none wasted or destroyed, the vibrations

gathered as a zillion finite particles into
this me, by the law of thermodynamics
destined to never end, just to become
changed, rearranged into another order.

Ask the physicist to explain. And believe.

Ireland is Here *by Noel King*

He forces his wife to beg on Westmoreland Street while he sits at home,
watching illegal TV coming from his home country, drinking special
  tea,

smoking incessant fags smuggled over by his brothers and nephews.
If she doesn't bring enough money home to the flat he slaps her

hard on the face, tells her she must keep Raisa in from school:
Raisa is pretty, show Raisa's pretty face and then they give money.

The mother wants Raisa to *get clever, a real job*, marry *whom she wants*.
Secretly she is putting money in an old biscuit tin under a floor board.

This will be Raisa's running away money, if one day she would need it,
then she might pick herself a new name, any name she likes.

On Westmoreland Street meanwhile, the wife continues holding her
  bowl out
but only till 12 noon cos in the afternoon she spreads her legs

for men of all ages in the massage parlour, spreads her legs
so that Raisa – the very one born from between hers – won't have to do
  so.

In the Finglas schoolyard the other girls don't play with Raisa.
Other girls have tried but the fact is Raisa just can't mix.

She can study, is well able to follow the teachers,
but sits all on her own, head down in the playground.

PE is torture for her: she won't change her clothes in front of the other
girls. At home in the bath Raisa folds her legs over,

when her mother comes in with another kettle of hot water,
is ashamed her mother will see the hairs starting to grow 'down there'.

On the Dodder Walkway, to the rear of the Aviva Stadium
Raisa sometimes accompanies her older brother in dog walking.

He earns pocket money dog walking for well-off fellas who work long
hours in Google. Sometimes, with quieter dogs he lets Raisa hold the
   leads.

The family in the flat over the wall don't have it so good,
the man there lets other men have sex with his wife,

they don't give him money but let him do the same to theirs.
They shout and fight and bang things a lot at night, keeping Raisa
   awake.

The girl in the flat over the wall is fourteen, used to hang around with
Raisa, but is too sophisticated now, is already having intercourse,

in secret, with a Protestant Irish boy of fifteen going on sixteen,
whose father franchises a Spar somewhere on the Southside.

The mother knows her sister in Tralee will take Raisa in
if Raisa needs to run one day, her mother keeps a secret

Irish Rail Dublin Hueston/Tralee timetable in the tin with the money
and a bag with essentials and even more in a trusted neighbours flat.

On Friday's after school Raisa goes with her mother
to the open laundry under the canopy at Centra,

they put the family's weekly wash into the large drum,
drop in the 4 x €2 coins and wait for the cycle to end.

And if the father one day asks the mother where Raisa is,
her mother will simply shrug one of her shoulders

and say: *Gone*. He can beat her
all he likes then.

Dockers, 1930 *by David Butler*

First light.
The descent from the tenements.
Flat-caps and donkey-jackets, shoulders
hunched against an easterly would skin you.
Keen-eyed, skint, eager for the scrimmage about
the rough pulpit to catch 'the read', the foreman
meting out who works, who idles.
A hard graft for the chosen.
Scant light
aslant through moiling
dust inside the dusky hold of a collier
where rope-muscled, calloused hands
rough-handle shovel-hafts, scraping, angling,
hacking irascible black-flecked phlegm until,
begrimed like pantomime blackamoors, they emerge
to carry their thirst like a wage and pay out
the bitter tithe - the match-boxed shilling
that buys the wink and nod.
It's that or starve.

Waiting for Gold *by Sheila Aldous*

From the red sky I saw goldsmiths
pouring twenty-four carats into the Teign.

The gold glinted on the heads of salmon
as they jumped in concentric circles.

Precious liquid melded together, made
a bracelet for the goddess of secret smiles.

The gold drew itself thin and wiry, a message
for a king from seven magpies

and the waters rolled with the honeyed tide
spreading out sheets for a mistress.

Closed lip of tors snatched the sun,
blinked the grey iron of a heron's wing.

The river died, a silversmith's eye
faced with the competition of aurelian fire,

as the gilded plate washed with darkness
was turned away in prayer.

I will keep watch, wait for the goldsmith
to return, to tell me the secret

never to be told, to lay out his sheets,
to cast me onto his bed of song,

and I will wait for the leaf of time,
the rounding, the gilding, the beaten path.

Mermaids, and where to find them *by Karen Hill*

If you believe the old stories
you will not find them in the likely places
rather in the unexpected

not in the ocean's grey-green depths
(which anyway are as shallow
as a drowning man)

not in dappled woodland pools
nymphs and naiads and naked young men

or astride a rocky outcrop, combing
bits of silver through their hair.

No, you will find them in dusty
churchyards, in the knaves of ancient
churches – faceless whorls in the wood

or tripping through the market-place
on borrowed feet.

My sister Bronwen found hers in a garden
pool, streaming pondweed hair and empty
stones for eyes – it was the day

our mother disappeared. Afterwards
she claimed an affinity with the
drowned, took to pulling soggy

cats from water barrels and walking
among the blanched bones of
sailers left carelessly on the beach.

She fleshed them out, gave them
bell-bottoms and a cocky smile

saw herself kissing away the brine

from their salt-smeared lips. Now
she sits counting the pearls in
discarded oyster-shells, waiting

for a sea-change to bring her
home. It has no choice – she
lacks the legs to run.

My mother's heart *by Phil Coleman*

My mother's heart's too tough
to stomach, cuts like old brown balls.
Stitched leather valves, cord-wound
muscle, sage and onion pursed.

For Sunday tea, gold-jellied tongue
sliced sandwich thin. Too rough a cow's
French kiss to swallow easily. It was always
Take one more before the cake got knifed.

She learnt offal in a poor kid's war
jackals scratching at the kitchen door.
Old man Jack loved livers, fried with onion
kidneys slippery with blood and piss

or sweetbreads poached in milk.
She often had just bread and scrape.
You can't let good dripping go to waste.
He drank the pennies, smacked her face.

The Archangel Dreams *by Peter Wallis*

Top of Gabriel's bucket list
is sex.
He dreams of having hairy legs,
a five o'clock shadow, Gillette,
a shed. He wants to sweat.

He wants to wear socks. Gabriel covets
a laundry basket,
walking boots complete with mud
and a springer spaniel.

The Archangel dreams of having kids,
doing the school run,
job interviews, and mates.
Hi chosen name is Dave.

He wants a wife,
who sometimes refuses him a kiss – *Your breath
stinks of garlic,
Whatever were you thinking of!*

So he dreams of sleep.
Gabriel wants to be *of colour;*
to buy Cadbury creme eggs,
and use the self-check-out at Tesco Express.

He wants to know what it is
to be time-limited
and to experience every bucket list's last wish,
A good death.

Ebb Tide, Morecambe Bay *by M. Valentine Williams*

Hest Bank.
The cocklepickers dig
out in the estuary,
apron of the cold, lap-slapping sea.

Razor clams lick tongues with cockles,
sinking in glutinous unwashed mud.
Covered in shell shucks,
lugworm spew their coils.

Here samphire holds the memory of land
on runnels oozing the dredge;
dry stickdrift sheaf piles scattered
on the tide's edge.   Motion suddenly,
the tide turns,
tumbles all around itself, filling in the flats.

Elephant grey; sand creases and folds,
crater pale,
topples. Pewter-puddled sea ribs
ripple.
Steps shake unsteady ground,
(quicksand of no turning back, not now, not ever.)

The siren sounds.

Caught in the sucking sinkhole of the sea
eighteen were lost,
sandmouthed and lead-full of water
as they waited, going down
for help to come
to the teenaged boys from Zelong Village
who will never go back home

The Red Kite *by Barry Norris*

One day my father took me to the nearest beach.
He urged wind into a red kite's skin, jabbing the string.
'It's up! It's up!' he shouted, like a seagull screech.

But the slackening string fell, a flopping filigree.
Increasingly miserable, each cast into the reluctant air
Just added weight to my father's kite-diving despair.

'There's just not enough wind. It will never fly',
He cried. But then, with astonished eyes, he watched
As I launched the red kite into the accepting sky.

And I, taut on the end of the strumming string,
Sustained the red kite upon the restless breeze,
My bird of prey, its wings quivering.

Not for a second did my rapt eye
Leave that shimmering bird. For in that moment,
I held the wind. I earthed the sky.

The 2020 Winners
Judged by Sally Spedding

The Debt Due *by Sheila Aldous*

I noted in that room
The absence of your life —
And yet its term of expectancy
The welcoming of the bloody cord
Your little body caked in vernix cervosa.
I note as I walk the paths of Cwmdonkin
The pleasure of earth
The sweetness of soil
The flowers having lived
Replaced with seeds like you.
I note the defiance
To beat the flesh
To berate the weakness
To take a fist to the body
To uphold the spirit of you.
I note the presence
In the absence, in the rage
In the knowledge in you
To know the wage of life is death.
And then too, I note your absence in the air
The breath of you subtracted in the gentle night.
I note the long cry of you
The honesty of you, the ghost of you
In the terrible of the day, in the drink of you,
Of what they said about you: a boy of summer in his ruin.
And your father, I note his absence —
For you his betrayal by death
The devastation of his absent steps
The allusion to his truth
The empty delusion of pain

The burning end of light.
And I noted you living in the absence
In the shadows
Unbaggaged on the journey
Knowing about the payment of the debt
Knowing about being born to die.

Dylan Thomas was born at 5, Cwmdonkin Drive, Swansea.

To Paul Celan *by Linda M James*

Forever touching the edges
of your words – their lack of answers –
their spoken silences.

Love in a tango of dark blue eyes.
In Poppies. In Remembrance.

You played with Bereicherung:
a reality richer than mine.

How could I cope with your language?

You ask: who would not linger in death
before mirrors? I ask: do fractured words
flower in the dusk of your smile?

Last night I broke your gazelle gaze
in a white forest hoared with Jews.
Serpents and daydreams mastered me:

Silence pushed the borders of pain
through thresholds. Stones screamed.
Mouths hid in mirrors.

Float me a second skin, Celan, so that
I sing in front of strangers – lighter
than the sky. Ballooned with words.

Unscythed *by John Gallas*

By Paparahi Flat, just past the droving bridge,
a vasty field of uncut corn rattles, torn,
sere and straggle-flapping, up to Bonners Ridge.

It's Winter now. I don't know why, in ragged rot,
this tall and stalky race were left uncropped, bereft
of use or profit, bluntly clattering, forgot

and draggled-pale, their shreddy leaves like flags,
their cracked confusion like a beaten, huddled troop,
abandoned, standing still, in August's rimey rags.

Their neighbour-whispers, nods and anxious wags betray,
it seems to me, some shabby incredulity
at some long luck, some higher husbandry that stays

their felling and their muddy end, some shrunk surprise
that they are left alone. I watch them gasp and click.
Their green-time gone, their salad-days long passed, they rise,

a little blankly, yes, a little like a crowd
achatter when the show is done and all the darkling
auditorium of earth an empty shroud

of wind and cold, but standing still. Perhaps this way
of dying, atom-slow, defying expectation
and the time, this easeful progress downwards, may,

with distant busyness, and blindness in the dark,
be mine. I leave the gate and cross the mudded bridge.
Above the track two slapping kahu wheel and cark.

I follow them to Brackall, past the flooded farm,
across the ice at Denham's Dip to Birthday Creek,
and then the rimus' shelter, and its sudden calm.

Judge's comments

It has been a huge privilege to have once again been invited by Dave Lewis to adjudicate this year's ever more prestigious and truly international Welsh Poetry Competition, with a record number of entries. The main themes involved memories, family and relationships, trees, flowers, woodland, birds, the sea and its shores, death, dying, hospitals, lockdown and its consequences, journeys, doom, pregnancy and birth, recollections, self-examination, Aberfan and other places in Wales. Other countries' histories, too. Save for one poem, there was a noticeable lack of humour, which is hardly surprising. However, a veritable treasure hunt, with so many gems to choose from...

My criteria: Instead of merely chopped-up prose, I was looking for musicality, assonances and alliteration etc. If rhyming, then subtle. Not everything spelled out, instead, leaving room for the imagination. Not narcissistic and self-indulgent. Too much interiority can be tedious. Originality of subject matter and its treatment. To be shown something I didn't know or been aware of. Interesting histories / countries / areas and revelations. Injustice and betrayal.

1st Prize – The Debt Due by Sheila Aldous

Inspired by Dylan Thomas' visceral and moving poem 'I Have Longed To Move Away' first published by New Directions in 1935, this is an achingly empathic revelation of the then young poet's need to break free from what he saw as entrapment between society's conventions and what he believed to be 'the lie' supporting them. Despite his need to be more true to himself and spurn what he felt to be damaging, the conflicted Dylan wasn't quite able to do this. And then in 1952 came his beloved father's 'betrayal' by death.

All this is captured by another accomplished poet who, it seems, is almost haunting 5, Cwmdonkin Drive, privy to Dylan's innermost thoughts and feelings. Whose last two lines say it all.

131

Knowing about the payment of the debt
Knowing about being born to die.

A tour de force and a worthy winner.

2ⁿᵈ *Prize – To Paul Celan by Linda James*

Forever touching the edges
Of your words – their lack of answers –
their spoken silences.
Love in a tango of dark blue eyes.
In Poppies. In Remembrance.

The first five lines of this spare, but evocative, questioning poem, introduce us to a gifted man born in 1920 in Romania to German-speaking Jews, who wrote under a pseudonym and whose second poetry collection, Mohn und Gedaechtnis (Poppy and Memory) established his reputation. Then came the well-known 'Fugue of Death' opening with 'Black milk of daybreak we drink it at evening we drink it at midday and morning we drink it at night' before an unsparing account of life in the Nazi death camps where his parents were killed and he was interned until escaping. Despite a later successful academic career in Paris, married with a son, Paul Antschel (his real name) committed suicide in 1970.

This 'tribute' ends with:

Float me a second skin, Celan, so that
I sing in front of strangers – lighter
than the sky. Ballooned with words.

A truly well-deserved runner-up.

3rd Prize – Unscythed by John Gallas

By Paparahi Flat, just past the droving bridge,
A vasty field of uncut corn rattles, torn,
Sere and straggle-flapping, up to Bonner's Ridge.

Straight in with a great title and vivid description of winter on New Zealand's North Island where the last words of this fresh, beautifully observed location sum up the scene with the end of the fifth stanza before the next one.

Their green time gone, their salad-days long passed, they rise,
a little blankly, yes, a little like a crowd
achatter when the show is done and all the darkling
auditorium of earth an empty shroud.

A well-deserved third placing, for a poem, which showed me another world far away.

Sally Spedding, July 2020

Organiser comment

Since the start of the contest, back in 2007 we've always felt it important to pick out as many poets as we can for admiration. We've been criticised over the years for having a 18th, 19th and 20th place etc. All I can say is that if one of my poems was picked 20th in such a competitive contest, packed full of some very accomplished and well-published poets, I'd be thrilled. This year was no exception and in fact our judge, Sally Spedding, felt that the quality of poems submitted this year was so good that she has also singled out a further five poems / poets that deserve a mention. They are as follows:

Boneyard – *Jennifer Watson*
Summerland – *Chrissy Banks*
The Speed Of Ice – *Partridge Boswell*
Pontypridd – *Jeanne Ceridwen Christie*
From St. Martha's Hill – *Lizzie Ballagher*

Special mentions

In addition Sally also liked the following poems / poets, who also should be identified. In no particular order they are as follows:

In memory of my father: upholsterer – *Philip Dunn*
The derelict farm – *Barry Norris*
Stallion – *Kevin Smith*
A recipe for rewilding – *Kathy Miles*
As the Rev Nicholas might have thought of chocolate – *L A Watt*
The headmaster, circa 1955 – *Judith Drazin*
When the trees were still dangerous – *Paul Nash*
The Facebook of Faiyum – *Partridge Boswell*
Mirror my lust – *Rose Hinton*
Alley days – *Chadleigh White*
Calligraphy – *Anne Connolly*
Bottom left-hand corner – *Rob Barnes*
Star dust – *Judith Drazin*
Whose voice? – *Anne Forest*

Following behind – *Michael Forester*
Stars in jam jars – *Christian Donovan*
Life on the inside – *Beverley Sutton*
Dunnerholm – *M R Peacock*
Inversion layer – *Jilly O'Brien*
Carpathian rhapsody – *Simon Tindale*
Planting out – *Susan Szekely*
Ring of Brodgar – *Diana Sanders*
Picking blackberries – *Anne McCrudden*
Twenty-six – *Rebecca Brown*
The race – *Val Ormrod*
Gus – *Jane Langan*
On the bus with the ex – *Gale Burns*
Caitlin – *Robin Daglish*
Coffee houses – *Lorna Liffen*
The owl, the pussycat and the shark – *Judie James*
Quintet – *Nora Bartley*
Bereavement – *Odette Short*
The gamekeeper's dogs – *A F Paterson*
Salt – *Jennifer Watson*
Residue – *Mike Douse*
Stillwatch – *Jackie Biggs*
Bardo – *Scott Elder*
Jane Eyre – *Philip Dunn*
Request stop – *Claire Lynn*
Gower Heritage Centre – *Charlotte Sanna*
Creirwy – *Paul Home*

Dave Lewis, August 2020

Specially Commended, 2020

Hidden Prey *by Sheila Aldous*

You ran wild once. Your slant of orange eye,
keen and watching, your dagger-sharp
teeth, pungent with the stink of killing.
Any prey would do in your scrabbling
to be pulled into a planned sarcophagus.
Any fence could be navigated, ripped,
scrambled, gnawed. No bird, hen, vole
or mole would escape. It was an art form:
a game before dinner.
Hidden, you watched the clock until
night fell, skirted fields sedged
and hedged, abandoned frequented
ways until the trap disguised of iron
and spike took you with leaves and twigs.
And you blared in the agony, whimpered
when forced to smell your own blood, before
you were clubbed until your senses made none
and you were dragged and rolled into a sack
to lie hidden in a pit already prepared and dug.
Until the day I surveyed my new land to build
a pond where I could play. I drew, sketched,
planned, priced the lot. I plotted a garden to be
decorated with ferns, rocks, stones,
fountains with water lilies to float on top.
I toiled all day, shoved in my spade until it moaned
and the soil was carved and aching. And then
it gave you up. I became obsessed, counted
your tiny fragments, your picked-over bones,
thought of all the ways I could display you.
Your ribs one way, femurs crossed and latticed
or lined up, your tail bones linked in a circle or
in a wide curve, your skull, devoid of eyes I wished
I'd seen, to be a captivating centrepiece.
I placed you in my gracious hall, on a wall, under
glass in a frame, and admired the portrait I'd made,

your avarice for the kill. I could smell the blood.
And in the ornate mirror, inherited
from my mother, my eyes squinted
orange in the sun.

Listen to Me I am Odile *by Judith Drazin*

I am Odile, the one in black,
Who lonely in her tower room,
Listens to the ceaseless hiss,
Of Northern winds and yet more
Sinister the silken kiss,
Of an enchanter's cloak, slowly,
Caressing each stone stair.
Pity Odile, the one in black.
My father's creatures come
And go. Strangely the slack
Mouthed, swarthy one is kind.
Only my father's concubine,
Jealous of his false love
For me, will slyly tweak
My hair and spill my wine.
When I was quite a child, with spite,
She pricked my arm, until the blood
Stained her white shift. Since then
I have not greatly cared for white.
I am Odile, do not
Despise me, shun me, for
I dance to ease the pain of
Those on gibbets left to rot.
I am the dark side of the moon,
I am your Lyonesse, I dance
Down hidden pathways to unseal
Your secret room. I am your
Seventh magpie. So
Remember me, I am Odile.

Cell *by Helen Cook*

She scrapes in her testament:
No, Mother, do not weep.
The wall is solid.
She finds a way to
make a mark

proof that she exists.

Breathing in breathing out
her heart a funeral bell
tolling her hours
she chants into the stone
Most chaste Queen of Heaven.

Her voice, a cell within a cell

a single living thing

of eighteen summers
now wintering
here air is stale
here light is barred
here torment exceeds the cold.

She scratches her will into slabs
that listen but are mute:
Support me always.
Support me always.

She seals with her name –
the one essence not defiled.

Inspired by Gorecki's Symphony no 3 Sorrowful Songs, 2nd movement

Circumnavigation *by Sharon Black*

I wear the countries I have visited:
they clasp my breasts and waist,
hang in wide pleats to my knee.

Each pastel patch sits clean
against the next, like an arm fits
to a shoulder, a pelvis snugly locks

into the sockets of the hips.
A blue sea laps the hemline.
At night when I unzip the back, release

the bow, wriggle it to my feet –
the countries blazon my nakedness
like fresh tattoos. And if you were

to peel away my skin you'd find them
etched on my bones: I can't escape
the people I have been, the places I've seen,

even those I just passed through –
the vendor's smile on a back street in Chiang Mai,
the Marrakech policeman who let me

take the station sofa for the night,
the flasher in that neat French village –
my blood runs with them. Look: this wound

when squeezed, leaks the Mississippi,
these wrinkles on my hands
are the riverbeds of Namib Rand.

Even my womb is mapped:
both my daughters have wanderlust,
can't wait to get moving.

A Kind of Music *by Isobel Thrilling*

Nobody told me the chemo-therapy ward
has its own orchestra,

cheeps and burbles play strings
along veins,
odd tones from exotic birds,
bubbles and trills,

add in
the mobile phones and voices.

Schoenberg would be charmed,
pleased by
the unpredictable pauses,
interstices, gaps,
where any wanderer can slip through
and cause
mayhem among the harmonies.

A new tone-poem for the Proms perhaps?

Total Immersion *by Konstandinos Mahoney*

Three days, a continent slips by; Dover, Brussels,
Munich, Belgrade, Athens. I'm mobbed at the station,
kissed, hugged, pinched, squeezed, Costaki!
Καρδιά μου! Χρυσό μου! My Heart! My Golden One!
We drive off like film stars in Granddad's limousine.

He takes me to pavement cafes, watches me scoff
honey cakes, flicks worry beads as he listens to
my anglo-flow, says he's never met a boy who
talks so much, asks mum if he can borrow me,
send me to college, learn Greek.

Baptism day, I stand six years tall in a font for
dunking babies, shy skinny schoolboy in white
underpants. Crammed underwater, I surface to a
slathering of olive oil, taste sunshine, soil, mum's
lettuce salads.

Dried and dressed; white shirt, blue shorts,
choir chanting, hearts crossed up down, right left,
right left, Granddad leads me three times round
in circles, then, gold crucifix flashing, out into the
dissolving blaze of Saint Constantine Cathedral Square.

Mother Goddesses of Netherby *by Susan Szekely*

(Tullie House Museum & Art Gallery, Carlisle)

One continuous stone hemline
and six sturdy feet; shawls draped
over shoulders. The middle one
holds a bowl filled with fat fruits.
The others steady brimming pitchers
against their hips. They could be waiting
for a bus to anywhere: Appleby market
(the heft of a pie, a truckle of cheese).
The school-run. Night out in Carlisle
(significant birthday). A hospital shift.
A visit to the food bank.
The stone glitters. Their heads
have been smashed off, so I must guess
at faces: frowns, crow's feet, dimples,
smiles warm and wide as ovens. All lost.
Their splintered expressions buried
in an untilled field waiting for the plough.

Moths *by Sheila Aldous*

She was painted black in that dark root.
The needlewoman in her spun a coat of silk
and while hidden away she thought
of the catwalk,
the sashaying.

In her closed world she busied herself
until she was ready to lift the corner
of the skin, its skirt fanning
outwards over the horizon
of a cloth seam.

She would never shine like her showy sister
but she had starved herself
until streamlined, to swallow instead
the caliginous clouds
in a dead night.

Then in the tree house she saw him:
his hands fidgeting moths as he sewed
stars into the hem of his wings,
preparing for his orientation,
drawing his map

of straight lines, fixing his latitude,
navigating the angle of his path
against the moon.
Then he saw her reach for the lamp
and he plummeted

spiralling out of course
into her circle of flame.
And for a moment
they danced together
into that strange encounter,
into the closet of light.

In the Gents at Graig Y Nos Visitor Centre *by Phil Coleman*

There's a mural of the water cycle.
Here you pee, follow the flow
around to the waste water plant
that discharges into the river.

By good design real sunlight falls
through high, frosted windows
onto the navy blue sea that
takes up the best part of one wall.

Trace the route of evaporation
up into clouds on the ceiling
(ignore the strip light and cistern miser)
until cumulus hits hills above cubicle doors.

Your breach condenses on the cold walls
rain misting down, blown by hand driers.
Once they meant global warming
but not now they're wind powered.

Damned in a drowned valley
high above the empty soap dispenser
fresh water is piped to a treatment centre
you passed back on the main road.

So into the taps and all over the floor
thanks to the lovely boys of Year Four
streams under the door, then down
the Tawe, to flood Swansea once more.

Delft *by Tanya Parker*

The wider the horizon, the less you fear. This is a place of huge skies and low clouds, of new town houses, confident stone. This is the painted scene. Come in.

A woman sits at the virginals. Her blurred face plays to a looking glass. Her chevalier in courtly black sings the tune. She is his accomplished wren, to be heard not seen. The artist sees both of them.

He paints from behind a lens, lent him by a draper of the town, a chamberlain he knows by sight. This is one he can spare. He cannot spare much time.

Closer now, closer still. In his private space, the chamberlain heats glass. Stretched to a whisker, broken in two, the tips he makes are the smallest yet. Magnified five hundred times, in one caught drop, little animals, little atomies. More populous than the crowded town, they run and swim and spin, angels on the tip of a pin, more devils than he can name.

Never near enough, his sons are wrapped in cloth. Four parcels of white silk under the elm tree he chose. Its muscles are their branches, their roots its veins. Seals unciphered, wax cups emptied of blood, their cells strengthen the earth.

So he awaits the dignitaries. The Russian tsar, the English king, dons of the Royal Society jealous of his monopoly. Fearing thieves, he trusts truth to secrecy. But no, it's his wife's tread on the stair, and with her his daughter, carrying carefully, in case he is thirsty, a glass of water.

The Prettiest House in the Street *by Rebecca Palmer*

i

overripe banana trees and a mulberry tree at the back fence purple feet
and the neighbours mango tree that hung over our side of the fence
garden hose boiled from the Queensland sun trampoline dance yellow
swing set ramshackle garden shed we were never allowed inside green
timber purple and yellow teenage dreams timber floors walls creak
gravel crunching separates us from the ominous voices over the fence
Frank and his son who came back from jail and lived in the caravan
weet-bix cards and home-grown oranges the old man gave to us
handmade gardens do-it-yourself shower in the tree for hot summer
days prettiest house in the street

ii

lights out power crackling radio static static candlelight dinner
spaghetti from a tin for the four of us milk crate table everything boxed
up or tied down windows taped large white crosses the trees
thundering menacing swaying in gale-force winds violent lashing
makeshift lake in the backyard huddled under the dining table a game
of monopoly half started

iii

displaced legless neat gardens no more aluminium face staring back at
us stolen key stolen memories who lives there now we will never know
mystery family paint it black and in our new pink brick shithouse we
had a resort style swimming pool to drown our sorrows

A nut roast has arrived *by Simon Maddrell*

every christmas since 2016
now that he doesn't
remind me of thirty years ago
now that he doesn't
remind me of the nut wellington
one christmas thirty years ago
the red wine gravy no consolation
for my red meat fiend
who loved to retell his horror
of being force-fed greens & grains like a cow
needing a balanced diet
for his cheese & his butter
of being force-fed greens & grains like a bull
needing a balanced diet
for those medium-rare joys
a nut roast arrives every christmas
now that he doesn't.

i.m. Stephen Owen (1967-2016)

Lizzie Pinches (Grandmother's Skates) *by Chris Kinsey*

You find them abandoned by the frozen lake.

The men are still at war
            and all week
                        mistress and children have squealed out in skeins
like earth-cursed geese
                flapping
                        jerking
                                    failing to glide.

Your rough fingers caress the foot-stock's smooth grain
                                        trace curving steel blades.

Frost bristles irresistibly.

                                    The world holds very still.
Cinderella of the sedges,
                you fasten the straps in a trice,
                            rise to the runners,
                                        steady yourself with an ash whip
                    catapult
                        onto the ice.

Three times you nearly spill your heart
                            to the glazed-over lily pads
until it beats for you hold it high.
                        Your spine lengthens
                                    hips drop,

ankles fuse with the blades
                    find poise,
                            propulsion,
                                    power.

Lizzie Pinches you've never known such ease
                                    spinning across the landlord's lake.

Your pirouettes around Swan Island
                                hold their score until the thaw.

Everything, that hour, rings like fine china
                                sings like the glass you polish.

Welsh bamboo *by Mike Pullman*

or pea shooters, that were never worth the effort.
But still they grow like buggery on rubbished banks
amongst the dog shit and rose bay by train tracks,
next to cleaned-up waters, and through chapels

that godforsaken and sheepish, cower low
until restored by the faithless few with money.
Deep down flooded and drowned, walkways swirl
up to the face and back in a warm breath whispered out

in a car park above next to Asda's. Shafts and paths two miles
below creak and pierce sharp with smashed glass,
rat bones and tins left from the last.
Laughter, swearing, and fears emerge forty years on from

streets now free of miners and God. Plastic windows,
coloured gardens, a new hospital and new river
submerge a past of dust and wagon, slag and steam
and Dad stuck suffocating on the hill.

Welsh bamboo aka Japanese Knotweed

Qasida in time slowed to the rhythm of cats *by Dena Fakhro*

I.   Day's orchestra of prayer and car-horns is muted
and all freight trucks still lassoed into pens
Even our Google location is suspended somewhere
between dust-devils and minarets
For these desert-miles extend for days, for weeks
when a world outside our front-gate is unhinged
The roof over our heads scant shield
from incubi, succubi, vampires and the jinn.

Each masked approach is alert to one danger
that for every ill-chanced date, a single host –
A pathogen – might fundamentally alter our humours
attach toxins to the briefest of greetings
While we await announcements, delay ceremonies
fret over vigils, fear more anointments, ragged
Crowns and numbers that leap between breath
and sighs, then transform test positives into prey.

II. On pause, we give form to the feline shadows
sliding up garden vines like arabesques
Endless are days when these cousins of lions
incline to stretch the perimeter wall elastic
Before holding still as sphinges
that guard lanterns and watchtowers
Our plot locked-down, a floating island
all villages, commerce, shopping-malls on-hold.

The clock slowed, we exchange watches for sundials
measure hours between bird-song and nocturne
As units: feeding time, excavations, ablutions
and brief homage to the deity of cats
Our silhouettes thinly veiled behind lattices
have learnt their habit of siestas in haze
Or draw refuge from sepia and shade under carriages
of disused cars, verandas and nature trails.

III. Her early years feral, she arrived seeking a cat's cure
and underfed; we named her Bathsheba
Since the shrug of her fur revealed blurred lines
of Persian pedigrees (and some local talent)
Although the lamps of her eyes piloted by sage
and gas-light that steered her into our camp
Still thrilled for a rumble; she stole bulbul eggs
from cradles of bougainvillea frames.

Last Fall, in rain, she drove up again unannounced
abandoned all that shine from the streets
That nightly touting for rough-trade, which
given her long-haired appeal, was easy
Put her gaming aside for home and comfort:
tuna, biscuits and a hairy-backed bathmat
Slung beside a box of Tide, a laundry basket
and one rusted Hotpoint washing machine.

IV. Still peeping-toms continued to scale up lamp-posts
waiting for blinds to drop, sleep-lights to dim
Followed her nightly pass along the interior wall
over obstacles coiled and sprung
So that, two-months gone, as jasmine ripened
to sweat and the oleander-bush shuffled in bud
She emerged from its bowels bath-heavy
grown too slow to catch flies and birds.

On damp grass irrigated by dusk, she cooled
her swollen belly, her labour unhurried
While each blade, whetted by near-equatorial heat
dimmed to green, dissolved to marsh
And we imagined those tiny lungs gestated
leaning into her organs, squeezing her flanks
Or huddling against the cage of her ribs
a jostling queue waiting for first breath.

V. When three flames in her eyes narrowed to pitch
a trio of kittens flexed their slippered backs
And mewling cries offered us signs for next season
sock-shaped and kicking, pitching against the first
Of nine lots, we wagered that hope might trump
adversity; three blown seeds – piebald, rust and ash
All rough-cut gems laid with care on tiles one
by one, as she polished the buds of minute tongues.

But last week the sky broke and our Eden cracked
when whip lightning lashed out and tore up night
Then, at the sound of thunder, fate flung a well-hung
rival in her path; the twins she hurled to safety
But, on pivot and turn, the bloodied prowler hooked
the third from her clasp slinging him into constellations
Clawed and shelled, the desecration complete, when
Death strung another hostage upon a sunken back.

Chosen for the Sea *by Jolie Marchant*

Hard backed and burly, fellers appear early
  in the morning sun.
Tough men of timber, linger
  in the shadow of death.
With reverence, noble oak is eyed.
Slant of fall is set.

Towering giant of liberty, stands rigid as
  saffron sunlight flickers above its crown.
A mosaic mantel of burnished leaves, gold and lime,
  freckled with frosted jade.
A kaleidoscope canopy.

Time is up for this puritan of the forest.
Cuts are angled, wedges knocked
  in blistered bark to counteract the arc.
Axe comes down with a whack, swings,
  attacks the unyielding king.
Spangles spark.

Saws released, frenzied beasts.
Metallic arms thrust reaching for the heart.
Jagged fangs grind into cuts as
  dust sprinkles onto razor teeth
  that grin, revealing their plaque.

A shudder's felt as nutrients melt.
Pulpy core resins and minerals leak
  from their cherished home.
Smarting gums and haunted hormones
  follow through sinewy subways.

At the bellowing timberman's call,
  bending boughs creak from limb to limb.
Scavengers fall from flaying branches that

157

tremble in the path of shadows.
There's a deathly pause.
The injured warrior tips the balance and waits
    poised on rooted toes.
Silently he hurls defiance.
Then roars.

His girth shakes, growth rings judder and flinch.
Crescendo of splintering cracks, snap.
A gasp, an expiring groan echo as he
    plunges and slams the ground.
Shockwaves raise his hulk, bounces back.
A heavy heart on trembling earth.

This hardwood king, felled, chosen for the sea.
Cherished and prized.
Within walls of ancient oak is his call,
    riding on waves to battle.

Large hotel *by Robin Muers*

Let's watch this man…
Key in hand, he's off to find his room.
A crossroads! No signpost,
an open cupboard, mops, three women
commiserating in a foreign language.
You're welcome, comes their chorus,
to The Labyrinth.

He has no true love…
So, no ball of thread to lead him home.
Must trudge through marathons of corridor
- a lifetime of artificial light – and search
for something counting as success – survival
perhaps, by chance, in spite of his past.
And now his final choice: turn left or right?

You're holding your breath…
A gasp: *My number's on that door!*
Inside: a drinks cabinet, massive bed, luxury…
But what about his food? (You scream out loud.)
No sweat, he says.   *"The One Percent Suite"*
includes the right to eat
the lost, the losers and
your bleeding heart.

The 2021 Winners
Judged by Kathy Miles

iii *by Estelle Price*

I begin with three.
Circular tub, grey pitcher, Mary
leant over, her alabaster chemise hung
like a bride's veil from peachy shoulders.

A wide window reveals charcoal sky,
allows the night's curiosity to rinse the attic
in glitter. At the canvas edge a solitary
curtain flushes. Will this do?

No, begin again. There is too much pink,
too much harmony. Mary, Mary, you should
be nude for the sake of decency.
Your navel's black stone

exposed, eyes cast down,
fingers busy with plaited hair. Let's cover
the floor with bruised sand, introduce
a vacant space

between your boyish thighs. The pitcher?
Take it away. Boiling water can't dissolve
the odour of this woman's desire.
The bath must

alter. Tip it up, let it open, mutate
to a single-minded orifice that gapes at the heart
of the composition. Or is it a ring?
A hoop of wedded-metal.

Enough. I'll finish with an arched window,
an urn set on a purple sill, artist's trap for a trio
of wilted tulips, two-red-one-yellow.
I end, I always end, with three.

(Vanessa Bell, The Tub, 1917, painting of Mary Hutchinson, Clive Bell's mistress.)

The Yellow Light *by Sheila Aldous*

The guttering candle is waxy in the yellow light.
A halo falls on his gaunt face, throws his long shadow
into the narrowing corner of the shit-walled cell.

The letter he is writing is blotted, torn with tears.
He wished he had not seen his mother yesterday.
She had grown old overnight. A body cancelled:

lined like Renoir's Old Woman accepting the dark.
He had admired that portrait, the debates with his students,
their essays on the light, the yellow light.

He feels his bowels slacken. A mute hope for leniency.
That somehow he will eject the stench of the sentence
like the reprieve winter gets sometimes from spring.

He waits for the priest who will mutter words of Christ's pardon.
He considers this barterer who will haggle without blinking
for his soul, for the promise of a fag and dinner.

He will be given the finest cutlery, whatever he fancies.
Not the woman though, he will decline that treat.
She would not charge of course: but fuss, cry, spoil it.

He cannot see the place it will be — the yard blanketed
by a ceiling of shawl-blue sky, drowning in the stain of blood,
but he'd heard the commands, the silences, the volley.

He had been told they would be precise, like swifts winging
through a black tunnel to the sun's yellow light —
that it would be quick.

*Patrick Pearse, a teacher, was executed at Kilmainham Jail, 1916 for his part
in the Dublin Easter Uprising.*

The Foundling Mother's List of Pain *by Jane Burn*

1. Walk, slow as you can towards that door
2. Cradle your child, feed on the scent of frail hair
3. Stitch the sight of new-born skin to the back of your eyes
4. Offer your miracle to somebody else's arms
5. Cut a hole in your clothes
6. Wear its wound, crave the missing piece
7. Breathe all your love into this poor scrap
8. Pray that time will not fret the kiss you press upon it
9. See your piece pinned into a sorrowful book
10. You will be bound by this inheritance of rags
11. Your womb will mourn
12. There is nothing you can do
13. Try not to feel the blade of years as they pass
14. Each blow of a candle, wear out the wish
15. Stop picturing your baby folded to your breast
16. Stop waking at night to imagined cries
17. Stop opening your palm to the ghost of tiny hands
18. Stop searching
19. Howl. Your throat is wolves
20. Every time a face peeps round the swoop of a skirt, look
21. Hold your breath and scry for echoes
22. You will probably never see your child again
23. Say *mother* and your mind will break
24. Grow old and never know

Notes: *Thomas Coram established the Foundling Hospital in London in 1739. It was the first children's charity in the UK. It still exists as a charity today. Tokens or pieces of fabric were left by the mother for her child in case at some point she could return to reclaim her child.*

Judge's comments

As a second-time judge for the Welsh Poetry Competition, I once again found myself humbled and a little overwhelmed by the huge number of excellent poems in front of me. Many good poems failed to make the final twenty simply because of the sheer volume of outstanding entries. Subjects were wide-ranging; lockdown featured of course, as did poems about nature, family, Welsh history and myth, climate change, and sadly, also many poems dealing with domestic abuse and the decline into dementia of a loved one. Whilst it was slightly disappointing not to see more pieces that dealt with contemporary political and social issues, I was surprised at the large number of ekphrastic poems submitted, all of which were exceptionally well written. Poems came in a variety of forms, from sestinas and villanelles to sonnets and free verse, and included a glosa, a golden shovel, a Viking lay, and a very funny rhyming poem, *'The Naughty Nit'*, sent in by nine year old Camilla Heitmeyer.

What I looked for in particular were well-crafted pieces that had that little bit extra; poems that made imaginative connections, which engaged completely with their subject, or where a slant viewpoint or strong narrative thread gave them a different perspective. All of the winning and Highly Commended poems have those elements in common. But every poet should feel extremely proud, because the work was of such a high standard throughout. It has been a real privilege to judge the competition this year, and I would like to thank Dave Lewis for inviting me, and all entrants for their great submissions.

1st Prize – iii by Estelle Price

I came to this poem without knowing either 'The Tub' or much about the complex triangles of Vanessa Bell's artistic and personal life; the subtext to the visual '*iii*'s of the piece. But from the start I was struck by the freshness and originality of the approach, and the way the poet engages wholly and intimately with the artist, and with her thought-processes as she revises the painting. The artist's feelings towards her subject – Mary Hutchinson, the mistress of Vanessa's husband Clive Bell – are made abundantly clear when she removes a pitcher from the composition:

'.....Boiling water can't dissolve

the odour of this woman's desire.'

The poem is a glorious and imaginative tale of revenge, as the painter quite literally strips her subject naked in the most marvellous and humiliating way: 'Mary, Mary, you should / be nude for the sake of decency', and changes the depiction of the tub to 'a single-minded orifice that gapes at the heart / of the composition.' There is cheekiness here, and more than a little touch of malice in the brush. It was also a refreshing change to see an ekphrastic poem written about a female artist. This is a beautifully-written and passionate poem, and is the one I kept coming back to over and over again during the judging process. An absolute triumph.

2nd *Prize – The Yellow Light by Sheila Aldous*

A powerful and memorable poem, *The Yellow Light* vividly captures the thoughts of the Irish nationalist leader and teacher Patrick Pearse as he awaits execution for his part in the Dublin Easter Rising. Again, the poet takes us right into the mind of his subject, as he writes a farewell letter to the mother he saw only yesterday: 'She had grown old overnight. A body cancelled: / lined like Renoir's Old Woman accepting the dark.' The imagery throughout is precise and intense, as he waits not only in the faint hope of a pardon from the authorities, but for

'...... the priest who will mutter words of Christ's pardon.

He considers this barterer who will haggle without blinking

for his soul, for the promise of a fag and dinner.'

The repetition of 'he' throughout, particularly at the beginning of the last five tercets, is a device the poet uses to emphasize the lack of control Pearse feels over his situation, and which serves to highlight the particular isolation and self-absorption of the condemned man in his cell as he hears the sound of his comrades being shot by firing squad. And a superb ending, which takes us right to the heart of Pearse's fears, and his hope for a swift death:

'He had been told they would be precise, like swifts winging

through a black tunnel to the sun's yellow light –

that it would be quick.'

A very worthy second place winner.

3rd Prize – The Foundling Mother's List Of Pain by Jane Burn

A good list poem has to work both inside and outside of the restrictions of the structure to avoid becoming merely a series of tropes or clichés, and *The Foundling Mother's List of Pain* does this brilliantly. Set in the C18th, it comprises a list of imaginary 'instructions' to a new mother who is forced to give up her baby to a foundling hospital. As the poet's note tells us, such mothers were allowed to leave a token of fabric, in case they were able to reclaim the child at a future time. The poem is a progression, starting with the moment of arrival at the hospital, where the poet guides both mother and reader through the process with a set of heart-breaking commands:

1. *Walk, slow as you can towards that door*
2. *Cradle your child, feed on the scent of frail hair*
3. *Stitch the sight of new-born skin to the back of your eyes*

We feel the mother's pain throughout the years, in language, which is simple and direct, but vividly paints a picture of loss:

16. *Stop waking at night to imagined cries*

169

17. *Stop opening your palm to the ghost of tiny hands*
18. *Stop searching*
19. *Howl. Your throat is wolves*

The grief of a mother for a child is timeless; these stages of loss bind the past to the present intimately and seamlessly, as do the directives, so reminiscent of the 'self help' guides of today, such as the 'Tasks of Mourning' models. A stunning poem.

Kathy Miles, August 2021

Special mentions

As always there were many other poems that our judge felt could have made the Top 20. So, in addition Kathy also liked the following poems / poets, who also deserve a mention. In no particular order they are as follows:

Shedding Wilderness - *Jonathan Greenhause*
the behaviours of sheep - *Lucy Crispin*
Listen to the sea-women - *Marion Oxley*
Ravel at Montfort l'Amaury - *Christopher M James*
Escapology - *Elizabeth Parkes*
Mud - *Ben Verinder*
Him outdoors - *Phil Coleman*
Skomer Island - *Stuart James*
Kamikaze - *Lindsay Pettifor*
First watch - *Anne Marie Connolly*
Day 109 - *Mark Fiddes*
The Stone Cottage - *Partridge Boswell*
Winefride - *Sheila Jacob*
Ecologue with my dad on Bradnor Hill - *Ken Evans*
The icon in Room 711 - *Denise O'Hagan*
Porth y Wrach – The Witch's Landing - *Alison Wood*
Hug - *Pratibha Castle*

Specially Commended, 2021

Shoes and an old woman who once lived in them *by Julia Usman*

Before I was your mother
I lived in kitten heels/ stilettos/ mules.
I was a woman with so many feet
I didn't know whether to laugh/ dance/ run wild,
so, I carried them all on the outside,
until I met a blind-date/ lover/ stranger.
My shoes would make small talk/ flirt/ lie,
but this lie/ half-truth/ misunderstanding,
attached itself to my sole as though
I had walked into my bruises
deliberately/ accidentally.   You see,
when I was young enough not to be your mother,
I believed in love/ true love/ happily ever after,
even though my shoes gave me blisters/
a split lip/ black eye,   because
the only fantasy/ fairy story / bull-shit
I failed to walk past, was the fist of a man
with a bankrupt smile/ large cash account/ ego,
who emptied my heart of shoes
and replaced them with his boots.
Now this old woman lives barefoot/ alone,
and the only shoes I own, live in a box/
a scar/ an empty bed, where I imagine
I am your moccasins/ your slippers/ your home.

Entertaining Caravaggio *by Julian Bishop*
(after Caravaggio's *Bacchus*)

The cardinal's cock-eyed, the Master's tired and emotional,
overdosed on Merlot and sun.
Back at the Palazzo I'm in a pretty state as we split a carafe,

arms charred as a martyr. I strip off my top, the cardinal whips
out emollients for the burn,
gestures to a divan, some dirty bed-linen as temporary robes -

he's not frugal with a soothing rubbing-down. The wine flows
like the Fontana di Trevi,
the Master grinds some white lead in a pestle *for your chest -*

I detect a painting coming on. The cardinal offers me a crown,
tiara of tangled vines,
rustles up a platter of rotting fruit. I look a picture - ribboned

in a toga with bows, I'm a panettone, a sweet treat to titillate
the cardinal's *inamorati.*
Bacchic on a grubby cushion, a chalice of fermented pleasure

ripples in my hot hand. I notice my nails need a good scrub,
I'm getting increasingly juiced.
For weeks, all I can think about is the cardinal's spoiled fruit.

Women of Birkenau *by Bex Hainsworth*

It is April when my mother and I visit the camp.
The cold womb of the world is thawing
and white flowers grow beside the railway tracks.

Our guide leads us to Block 25,
where women were shelved, twelve to a bunk.
Filthy, starving, scratching at their skeletal armpits,

but still, alive. *Lager Schwestern*, when the SS marched
their families into ash, they reached out to each other,
like roots beneath the earth, spreading, secretly, in the dark.

An extra ounce of turnip, a familiar *klezmer* tune hummed
like a lullaby, a coin of bread, rumours heard in radio static,
dirt-printed fingertips stroking bristled heads.

The daughters of Sarah and Rebekah and Leah
took up needles fashioned from wooden splinters
and thread from lice-stiffened sheets.

They stitched together not a shroud, but a blanket
for the baby, whose mother gave birth in a wagon,
leaning against a pile of corpses.

Others carried the emptiness around with them: a hollow relief,
doubly-sentenced, but left wondering at their bodies, stopped
like pocket watches piled with the precious things in *Kanada*.

I stand in their absence, touch the wood and stone of their beds.
The light from the square window at the end of the barracks
is turning the grey dust to gold and as we leave, I picture the women,
staggering out into the sunlight, the blood dripping between their legs.

This shy architect *by Dena Fakhro*

Instead of ordinary walls
       or even the yawning space of executive luxury
here stretches an iron-spoked umbrella bridging its back
from bank to bank;
a canopy with stone-carved wings fanned

onto a halo of Victorian architecture.
And bedded on straw at the end of this rainbow
is a ragged bather – sun-burnt but positioned in shade
and within spitting distance of some aluminium can-tabs
filters and butts that tell of both his

and others' expended gratification
and which shimmering under lamp-light
might form the shells of his shore.
Here lives Leonardo; another shy architect
self-styled and while inspired by his namesake

both his own creator and the subject;
a Vitruvian man pinned onto slate like a star
though those under shelter see a vagrant born a snow angel
on winter nights when he is victim to the track
jolted and charged by a reverberation of trains

after drifting to dreams under the station clock.
When he wakes he witnesses the shape of things to come
for some days he even floats
and becomes a boat man passaging the living
but on fitful nights his clouded eyes part and note

with that unique sensibility gifted to those caught between worlds
those who won't make the crossing.
He lives open plan, caged in plain sight
this home and garden cover-worthy
and buffeted by bubble wrap, discarded packaging, stained blankets

and mould on cartons that wrinkle at the prospect of rain.
One man among the homeless, he sits, sleeps, eats, reads about the big
  issues
and performs a litany of ablutions on or near an installation
that a Nordic lifestyle store might one day customise for city living;
at needle point he even speeds like German automation

drugged and stunned, never and forever moving
St Paul's always in sight and the river bleeding to distance.
He lives where a platform camera turns on a dime
fine-tuning the station-keeper's gaze with an intimacy or a daily
  reproach
– sharp, square-eyed, snapping him back into focus.

Modigliani Answers His Critic *by Sheila Aldous*

It is true – I paint in a hurry. I stand accused —
my hand denies individuality, my greed for art
sucks potential, replaces their fame with mine.
What can I say, I am their master, but they dress me
in a fever: these peasants, street girls, flower sellers.
I am caught like my brushes, colouring in my own folly.
Such is this: they sit, recline, smile, place
their hands, just so. Their tapering fingers long
to touch canvas, the gilded frames, to stroke the oils.
I cannot but draw them into me. Each pout, a smile
of a cupid bow, kisses me; and it matters not if they
are men or women, they bequeath their breath to me,
endow me with their secrets. You will see my addiction
this peintre maudit, frequenter of bars, boulevards,
in my joie de vivre, in the boudoirs, in my soul.
My models do not laugh, but interrogate, penetrate
with serenity; with eyes one blue, one grey, ask nothing
in their elegance, just whether they sit, or stand, or lie down.
And yes, they are me and I am them. My nudes,
you say — well, what of them? They are the perfection
of a world bracing itself: a curl of pubicity
this triangle that shocks the mesdemoiselles et messieurs
parading with parasols in the parks, mannequins of Paris.
Oh, so disapproving — but so all-knowing.
Whether my models are fully dressed in the finest
couture, in the undergarments of a paid putain
or in their own skin, the alabaster light plays on.
Do not say they disappear like fog into this spectacle,
that I am a wastrel who stretches necks, for I pour them
elongated like bottled wine into my blood.
You ask if I care for them: of course, this press of creation
are my lovers on canvas, they are frisson at my fingertips.

Consoling the Whims of the Tiniest, Whiniest Dictators
by Jonathan Greenhause

My 5-year-old hurls school buses at me, tosses meteors,
catapults snorting hippopotamuses, squeals

This spells doom!!!, rails I'll never get away
with my malfeasance, my maleficence, my frequent use

of underarm deodorants, isn't quite sure
what deodorants do, irately summons the Nordic gods,

then charges like an ice cream van
zeroing in on a football practice's aftermath,

hangs from my hips like a stunted jackal,
like a mosquito administering its lethal dose of malaria.

I launch him through the stratosphere,
satellites whizzing by his orbital body, the winking moon

grazing his Spiderman pyjamas as he somersaults
into our sitting room, seizes our frantic terrier,

gallops in full armour towards his playroom fortress,
his baby brother still too young

to appreciate the deadly seriousness of fantasy,
even as he beams so broadly at the older one's approach

it's as if he were a Little John
witnessing Robin Hood's reincarnation. Soon,

these nippers will team up to attack their old man,
will wage epic battles of sofa cushions,

but first they'll bare their milk-white teeth,
will howl like wolves & swear that I'll never escape alive.

The Milkmaid *by Sally Russell*

In response to 'The Milkmaid' by Johannes Vermeer.

At dawn I am in the cattle shed, milking Gertrude,
skirts bundled up, free of cow pats and straw.
I sweat and pull at her teats. Her stench engulfs me.
A half-bucket is all she releases—
it will do for the master's bread pudding.

I scuttle across the yard to the cool kitchen,
an eye open for the master.
I drop the latch on the inside of the door.
The master has provided a foot warmer—
he likes to place it under my dress.

Sunbeams splash the walls with light;
apple tree branches play shadow puppets.
Baskets of stale bread await my attention.
I roll up my sleeves, adjust my white cap, push
cerulean skirts to the side. I lean into the table.

I grip the handle of the jug, steady its weight. Warm,
sweet milk trickles into an earthenware container. As I stir
the pudding, my thoughts wander to my master's
duck-down quilt, the tumble between white sheets,
scent of my mistress on the pillow.

Rebel Song *by Jean James*

(after Allen Ginsberg)

I heard the howl of those
who leapt the barricades with pails of ash and daubed the lodges with
    an epitaph,
who shut their mouths and slashed their wrists on razor wire curled on
    the prison walls,
who rode in long cars through the night to stash Kalashnikovs in secret
    bunkers,
who fed the bullets to the guns that shattered kneecaps of the white-
    gilled boys in terraced streets,
who stalked the fields in every weather marking the paths of quiet
    policemen and their blameless dogs,
who fed the fever for a promised land of milk and honey to the
    favoured few,
who blew up cafes, pubs and boardrooms breathing in blackness as
    they roared away,
who torched the curtains of the theatre scorching the watchers in the
    wings,
who handed money over counters wrapped in slack cloth and scarlet
    ribbons,
who faded out on bar room tables caught in the neon sequined lights, a
    trail of butt ends, shattered glass and everywhere the broken stools
    and empty cartooned floor,
who lost their way in lock-ins singing rebel songs and shoot the heroes
    for their tarnished medals pinned on chest bones in the rattling boxes
    they went home in,
who vanished swiftly into doorways and wrote about the good old
    days,

then sat, like old men on park benches, reading the suffering carved in
    stone.

A mural for 'Kitty' Wilkinson *by Philip Dunn*

Liverpool's Saint of the Slums.

A mural on Catherine Wilkinson
Would magnify the treasured civic tale.
What colours though for the wash house saint?
In chapel stained glass windows we've a guide.

Think blue for her mangle, her cellar boiler, bronze,
And caustic white for the chlorinated lime;
Then the Georgian slums, the Cholera year,
And Provident house – her blessed laundry.
She would be late at times with laundered sheets:
And may have been a final visitant
In Clontare Court, Cook's Court, or Gladstone Street.

Three washed-out women might well form the scene?
It can't depict their family's shared clothes:
One has boiled six shirts, four bed ticks* are next;
Some chaff left in the ticks lies on the floor.
And they had neither possing sticks or pegs.
They'd hardly have a crystal stream or hedge.
But render these as emblems centre stage:
The hallowed running water – not from the pump,
Three tubs, the drying lines, and kitchen stove;
And at its heart, her door in Denison Street.
Her tell-tale hands, what might be made of those.
What have they done with toil and suffering.

I'd want to hear her Derry tones, her words
On savings schemes and mending bath house towels
And Protestant pride; but we scarcely have her life.

* *tick: a mattress stuffed with straw.*

Lick and Split *by Sally Russell*

A Golden Shovel after Gwendolyn Brooks 'One Wants a Teller in a Time like This'.

She combs my hair, smooths my skirt, tells me, *Stand up straight.*
On with my scarlet beret for a photo on the porch. Round-shouldered,
I shuffle down the street, past the lake, tranquil
in September morning light, my progress eyed
by local lads sitting on a chip shop wall. The knowing
glances, pushing of phones into back pockets. One
with Iron Maiden tatts comes over. *Whatcha got there?* He knows
I'm scared. *Y'know what? We'll play splits. For*
every throw of my knife, you get a wish, he said. *Oh, sure,*
I thought. I stood, feet apart. He slid his knife from the
sleeve of his jacket. Made to lick the blade the way
he'd lick a lover. Zap. Knife between my feet. My turn. I back
away, take aim. Zap. Through his foot. How they taught me in the
home.

Becoming a Saint in Ely: a speculative life *by Pamela Job*

The wind off the fens finds the marrow of my bones.
I watch the sun break through to manufacture light

And, in this, her place, I think of Aethelthryth, her dessication,
whose bones failed to find flesh to hold them.

She fled here – far from warring men blinding this same sun
with metalled shields – in the midst of the riddle

Of an age when minds were filled with eels, when demons
in their saints' disguise infested people's dreams.

For her, the idea alone of God put flesh on faith at last.
Offered fine linen, she declined. She rationed hot baths.

But surely she would have wanted to get under the skin
of a day such as this, her eyelids closing on blue

on her way to bliss. Perhaps her strong belief turned each chill breeze
into the scant caress she scorned from men.

Always fasting to purge evil thoughts, did she think she was
withstanding well the state of weightlessness?

Her possible pleasures – we know she had no appetite for husbands,
for, *someone who is tied up cannot run,*

but she devoured books. Words, hand-wrought, freed her mind
to roam, a *highly ingenious bee in the flowering fields of scripture,*

so she was well equipped to recognise her soul when it skipped
towards her singing, *O I will leape up into God…*

Aethelthryth falls back into the shadows cast on a wall, as I retreat
to wrap my hands around the answered prayer of hot coffee.

187

Note:

Saint Aethelthryth, (636-679)

Words in italics: Evagrios of Pontus, (345-399); Aldhelm of Malmesbury, (639-709); treatise 'On Virginity'; Edith Sitwell, 'Still Falls the Rain'

The Rev'd Thomas with Scythe, Manafon *by Ross Cogan*

The gaunt, tall man, black clad

with just a line of white at the neck

like a bird's wing flash, bends

low over the scythe. Too low.

Unlearned limbs, a narrow back, above

all a mind that won't stop

imposing itself between the ebb

and flow of the blade's tide,

conspire to blur his lines and the scythe

stutters over tussocks like a tongue

blunted on alien vowels.

Unlike Prytherch, whose learned hands

belie his face's blankness, the parson

never could write a fine edge onto steel

with the whetstone, so he chewed

the churchyard grass instead

of cutting clean, or else trampled it

and like sly old sins under God's

roller, it rose again in the first rain.

And rain here is never long absent.

The grass, crouching beneath the belfry's hour hand

shade, or clumped round the date-stamped

stones, will endure. It will send its white roots

alike into the thin soil of the hills

and the rich, river-soaked loam

of the valleys and dumbly defy time

and humanity and even the blunt

machines of the godly, for it too

in its unshaven impudence

is a winner of small wars.

My Shameless Lips *by James Knox Whittet*

Verbal melodies flooded through my mind
when I was a girl. It was as if I was a burn
for truths and music. Village elders frowned
on me claiming that I brought shame upon

the clan but I went on composing in secret.
I bent my ear to whispers of winds as they
formed pathways through stoned fields of oats.
Each stilled evening, streamered with peat smoke,

I caught tunes out of the very air. The roar of
lusting stags in autumn found its way into
my verse. When departing tides left their
concentric rings on shell sand, I beachcombed

poems like salt sieved driftwood. I waulked
words as my mother waulked the urine soaked
wool when she joined her voice in wave after
wave of wailing song, wrenching music out of cloth.

With a creel of seaweed on my back, chilled salt
water, dried by sunlight, crusting around my neck,
I hummed words like leaping salmon psalms
under my breath. It was as if my people spoke

through me even though I was just a woman.
I was the voice of love, exile and drowning;
the voice of the curlew calling from bouldered
moors with the bog cotton dancing licentious jigs

around the hill lochans that wore their necklaces
of moonlight like shy brides. My brother joined
me in this conspiracy of song. They would not teach
me to form scrawled words on paper so I sang

191

and he regimented my silenced words in lines
like soldiers on parade. I grew bold through time,
I stood up in ceilidhs – they could not stop me -
and cast my words like nets around the centre

circle of glowing embers. I spun out my years
with the healing gauze of my poems until death
dumbed my voice and now I lie with my shameless
lips pressed to the earth as to a dark lover.

If you look closer – come, look at me closer -
you will see my lips still mouthing words,
striving to speak for the dead as I spoke for
the living: creating beauty out of loss and dirt.

*It was traditional for female Gaelic poets and song writers in the Scottish
Highlands and Islands to be buried face down after death as a punishment for
usurping the male role of Bard.*

To waulk is to stretch cloth in the making of Harris tweed.

Daughter of the Sea *by Miriam Mason*

a re-imagining of a Welsh folk tale

She ran past lines - the snap and sting, *white wings* -
and down past fences bent and houses with closed faces,
past gaping Sundays fished out with a spoon
and lazy limbs curled round.

She chased the sea's roar like a kite:
wild brew of gods wet-faced
this day, this diamond day, that bellowed with the gulls
all robbing beaks and battered cod and diving for the catch
as deckchairs billowed on the prom,
awaiting grey-haired sleep and toes spread thick with buttered sand.

Watch the mouth of envy howl.

forget
the stormy
afternoon, it is

this moment
when the wave erupts and
carries her through

mirrors, downwards,
backwards, black
as coal,

ballooning, silk
and blowing
jelly-like,
a spattering,
bright beads,

the suck and

spew of
waiting, slick between
the reeds, beware the
stab of spines.

We are the fish in the tank, my sisters.
I see the patterns cast by constellations of the stars and through the glass I see
a floating moon.

Toe in a stream tinkling, slip slip silver tears.

She can't remember who she was but she can feel the sky blush pink
upon her cheek.
She can't remember where she lived but she can hear a heartbeat falling
on the grass
and she can hear the wind:

firetail, nighthawk, falcon, kingfisher, curlew, kite
firetail, nighthawk, falcon, kingfisher, curlew, kite -

the eggshell eye cracks first.
beak dipped in yolk, steel hooks and razor curves,
skin sewn between the bones.
prehistoric.
pirate.
Gull.

Watch my wings as I rise up.
I'm inside out, the ghost of dragon clouds.

Between the land and sea she flies.
The scattered relics of a tribe and all the thoughts she ever had unwind
behind her.

Steatoda *by Mark Totterdell*

The kitchen window mortise, under the nose
of the cast iron rat tail handle, is her bolt-hole.
She's extruded a pale miracle of architecture,
fixed by fine struts to pane and painted wood.
She appears each evening, pendent, motionless,
neat as a button on a sheer silk sleeve,
awaiting a suitor, or supper. She could live for years,
a small dark grape with eight tapered stalks.
The only time we saw her shift was when
the big wasp fuzzed in and enmeshed itself.
We witnessed the bloodless kill, the tight shroud,
saw how she served us as she served herself.
We'll live with her, unless one careless opening
of the casement in spring should make a squidge
of spider guts, a stain of wasted venom.

Blood Lines *by Gwen Williams*

he pulled through at dawn
with the waking song of blackbirds
and a soft rain soaking the earth.

A fox lifted its head from the litter bin
as if it knew from the animal cries
a boy was not so much arriving

as being rescued like a soapy calf
roped and dragged by the hooves
out of its mother.

               A line of blood
marking his round cheek. A crusty eye
opening on a tender audience smiling
at the family chin the wisps

of ginger hair as time rewinds
to his brother's birth
to his mother's birth
to his father's birth

a feeling of chambered hours
reels back to other thresholds
three worn steps to a doorway

into a narrow corridor
where cots and coffins
winding sheets and shrouds

and swaddling clothes
are bundled into a loop of dusks
and dawns to be pulled through

Index of titles

A Clock Full of Coal by Neil Gower 74

A Kind Of Music by Isobel Thrilling 144

A Mural For 'Kitty' Wilkinson by Philip Dunn 185

A nut roast arrived by Simon Mandrell 152

Abandoned by Jackie Biggs 103

According to Dai by Vicky Hampton 70

After Easter by Aoife Mannix 67

Airlings by Rae Howells 5

All things bright and beautiful by Judith Drazin 65

Becoming A Saint In Ely: A Speculative Life by Pamela Job 187

Bergamask for the Neoplatonists by Mick Evans 23

Blood Lines by Gwen Williams 196

Bluebeard by Helen May Williams 47

Bob Dylan awaits for the Ferry at Aust by Deborah Harvey 99

Bones, not human by Caroline Davies 25

bonnie dearie by Sighle Meehan 83

Breaker by Louise Wilford 66

Cawl by Mari Ellis Dunning 36

Cell by Helen Cook 142

Chatter and Requiem by Dena Fakhro 63

Chosen by the Sea by Jolie Marchant 157

Circumnavigation by Sharon Black 143

Colouring in the Elephant by Sue Moules 81

Consoling The Whims Of The Tiniest, Whiniest Dictators by Jonathan Greenhause 181

Daughter Of The Sea by Miriam Mason 193

Delft by Tanya Parker 150

desert sculpture by Mick Evans 38

Division of the Chaff by Sheila Aldous 72

Dockers 1930 by David Butler 116

Ebb Tide, Morecombe Bay by M V Williams 122

Entertaining Caravaggio by Julian Bishop 176

From Vivienne to her Tom by Helen Cook 79

Frost at Lighthouse Beach by Partridge Boswell 105

Grip by Mick Evans 45

Hare on the lane by Louise Wilford 19

Heft by David J Costello 53

Hidden Prey by Sheila Aldous 139

iii by Estelle Price 163

In the Bowes-Lyon Museum by Pat Borthwick 33

In The Gents At Craig-Y-Nos Visitor Centre by Phil Coleman 149

Ireland is Here by Noel King 114

Large Hotel by Robin Muers 159

Lick and Split by Sally Russell 186

Listen To Me I Am Odile by Judith Drazin 141

Little Pinches (Grandmother's Skates) by Chris Kinsey 153

lost poem by Mick Evans 29

Making and Mending by Gill Learner 100

Marked by Trudi Petersen 106

Mermaids, and where to find them by Karen Hill 118

Modigliani Answers His Critic by Sheila Aldous 180

Mother Goddess of Netherby by Susan Szekely 146

Moths by Sheila Aldous 147

My mother's heart by Phil Coleman   120

My Shameless Lips by James Knox Whittet   191

On watching a lemon sail the sea by Maggie Harris   8

Otters by Gareth Writer-Davies   31

Prayer to a Jacaranda by Judy Durrant   51

Qasida in time slowed to the rhythm of cats by Dena Fakhro   156

Rebel Song by Jean James   184

Rough Magic by Noel Williams   40

Running by Natalie Ann Holborow   34

Sestina: The Boxer by Alex Hancock   110

Shoes And An Old Woman Who Once Lived In Them
  by Julia Usman   175

Skimmers by Jane Burn   7

Speak by Gareth A Roberts   108

Steatoda by Mark Totterdell   195

Sunflower Encolpion by Mara Adamitz Scrupe   21

Swansea Son by Laura Potts   85

Ten Minutes by Natalie Ann Holborow   17

The Archangel Dreams by Peter Wallis   121

The art of moving a piano into an upstairs flat by Kittie Belltree   27

The Boiling Point for Jam by Lynda Tavakoli   78

The Debt Due by Sheila Aldous   127

The Devil's Shoes in Back Home Afro-Caribbean Shop
  By Pauline Plummer   91

The Enchantment of Maps by Jean James   101

The Foundling Mothers List Of Pain by Jane Burn   166

The Map-Maker's Tale by Damen O'Brien   89

The Milkmaid by Sally Russell   183

The Mole by Jean James   54

The Party by Laura Solomon   84

The Prettiest House in the Street by Rebecca Palmer   151

The Promise of Elsewhere by Louise G Cole   112

The Red Kite by Barry Norris   123

The Rev'd Thomas With Scythe, Manafon by Ross Cogan   189

The Wren by John D Kelly   41

The Yellow Light by Sheila Aldous   165

Thessaloniki Station 1943 by David Crann   69

This Shy Architect by Dena Fakhro   178

Thorsteinsskàli, Iceland by Christopher M. James   75

To Paul Celan by Linda M James   129

Top Corris by Zillah Bowes   43

Total Immersion by Konstandinos Mahoney   145

Unscythed by John Gallas   130

Waiting for Gold by Sheila Aldous   117

Wearing Silk Pyjamas in an Aldershot Hotel by M V Williams   77

Welsh Bamboo by Mike Pullman   155

What are you owl by Rob Miles   93

where he lay undiscovered by Deborah Harvey   82

Women of Birkenau by Bex Hainsworth   177

www.welshpoetry.co.uk

'The First Five Years' is a distinct yet varied expression of the world we inhabit. Experimental, vibrant, musical, shocking, unapologetic. This anthology is as much for the unseen writers as it is for the commemorated. All art is opinion and all rules are meant to be broken. So if we have pushed a little further back the conventional and the humdrum, if we have shook up the establishment a little and injected life back into one of the greatest art forms available to mankind then we stand guilty as charged. That was indeed our intention.

'Ten Years On' is a celebration of the best poetry submitted to the Welsh Poetry Competition between 2012-2016. A diverse look at the world we inhabit – alive, energetic, melodic, unrepentant and moving. This anthology is for all poets who truly feel. For the brave, the feisty, the exuberant, the outrageous and the rule breakers. A chance to revel in the moment and not be afraid.

Published by
www.publishandprint.co.uk

Printed in Great Britain
by Amazon

78794604R00122